AF668470

Fatehpur Sikri

Fatehpur Sikri

Akbar's Magnificent City on a Hill

Subhadra Sen Gupta

Photographs Prakash Israni

NIYOGI
BOOKS

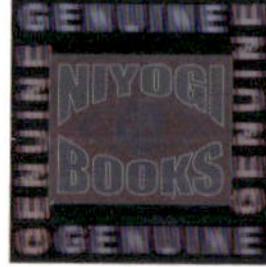

Published by

NIYOGI BOOKS

D-78, Okhla Industrial Area, Phase-I
New Delhi-110 020, INDIA
Tel: 91-11-26816301, 49327000
Fax: 91-11-26810483, 26813830
Email: niyogibooks@gmail.com
Website: www.niyogibooksindia.com

Editor: Jyoti Kumari / Niyogi Books
Design: Spiritnoise

ISBN: 978-93-81523-72-8
Year of Publication: 2013

Printed at: Niyogi Offset Pvt. Ltd., New Delhi, India

CONTENTS

INTRODUCTION

Introduction

The best time to discover Fatehpur Sikri is on one of those mellow, misty mornings of early winter in North India. Starting the journey as the first rays of the sun begin to lighten the sky, edging the clouds with a splash of pink and the birds soar upwards, welcoming the dawn like devotees of the sun god, Surya. The air will be fresh and chilly against the skin; as one's mind is filled with the anticipation of discovering Akbar's magnificent city on a hill, the legendary Fatehpur Sikri.

Fatehpur Sikri wears many faces. It captures that elusive blend of a king's love for royal pageantry and his philosophical quest for the meaning of life. It was a royal capital, a centre of art and culture and at its spiritual heart there is a Sufi dargah that has drawn Muslim and Hindu pilgrims for centuries. It was built as an act of thanksgiving for the blessings of a saint that gave a king a long awaited heir. This was the city of Jalaluddin Akbar who was a warrior, conqueror, empire builder and a superbly inventive king. He was also a man who questioned the certainties of formal religion and searched for answers along the thinkers of his kingdom. He relished not just the aspirations of the world but also the subtle searching of his soul. No other medieval city in India carries the stamp of its creator like Fatehpur Sikri.

Akbar's city of dreams deserves one's undivided attention and a spirit of curiosity and adventure. The Archaeological Survey of India lists over seventy monuments here, so there is much to see and savour, not just opulent palaces and arrogantly rising gateways but a lotus pool where a great singer sang to his king and the serene mausoleum of a Sufi preacher

◄ *The first view of the dargah of Salim Chishti through the Badshahi Darwaza.*

who lived a simple, ascetic life of prayer but now lies surrounded by luxurious marble. At Fatehpur Sikri, among the silent courtyards, shadowy palaces and by the carved pillars, Akbar's spirit still pervades the air. He is the ever present spectre in his ghostly city, a benign, regal presence you can sense everywhere. He was familiar with every building here, he wandered about as it was being built and even worked beside the architects and craftsmen. Then he sat dispensing justice from the Diwan-i-Aam, greeted foreign envoys in the Diwan-i-Khas and climbed to the top of Panch Mahal to enjoy the monsoon breeze. Fatehpur Sikri is the first planned city in medieval India and its designer was a king. As historian Milo C. Beach says, it was 'built during the most innovative years of his reign'.

In the sixteenth century this was the premier Mughal city, admired for its rich citizens, noble mansions and colourful bazaars but that was a

▲ *Stars, bells and inverted lotus: An elegant blend of Hindu motifs used across Fatehpur Sikri.*

long time ago. Agra was forgotten when Akbar's grandson Shah Jahan shifted his capital to Delhi in the seventeenth century. During the British Raj it was a cantonment town, what was called a *moffusil*, and today it lives for the tourists coming to see the Taj Mahal. Somehow the presence of the Taj distracts visitors from the magic of Fatehpur Sikri when in many ways it is a much more intricate experience. Agra and Fatehpur Sikri lie in the plains of the River Yamuna and the great Ganges flows to the east. The landscape is flat with an occasional hill near the horizon and it is the most fertile part of North India. Everywhere there are neat fields and large shady trees, orchards of mangoes and giant banyans letting down their roots to the ground and the spread of margosa with their narrow, bitter leaves and dappled shade. Everywhere you will see the myriad gifts of a generous, fecund earth. Today little remains of that Mughal presence except an occasional *kos minar*, the pyramidal stone milestones or a patch of a wall that may have once been a serai, an inn. Here carved sandstone pillars prop up tiled roofs of a village home, a mosque has a slender marble minaret and children play by a nameless grave in the shade of a tree. Somehow the landscape still carries the memory of those vivid Mughal times.

This ancient land has seen human habitation from pre-historic times. Here archaeologists have found Neolithic rock paintings and Rajputs have cultivated this land from the time of the epic battle described in the *Mahabharata*. The land has grown wise and cynical seeing the ups and downs of history, watching with all knowing eyes the puny ambitions of men, the invading armies and the builders of cities. They all come and go but what remains is the flowing river, the Brahminy kites wheeling high up in the sky and the ever changing seasons. Only a few leave their stamp on the landscape, one was a king and another was a reclusive Sufi saint. And they left behind a city that became frozen in time.

Long before the Mughals

The origins of the name Sikri go back far. Archaeologists exploring here, have found evidence of human habitation that go back to 1200 BC and it has been continuously inhabited since then. In the epic *Mahabharata* it is called *Saik* or an area surrounded by water and that could probably be a lake. They have found the remains of a Jain temple, where the inscription dates it to 1010 and calls the place *Sekrikya*. In the second millennium, before the arrival of the Muslims, this region was ruled by Rajputs. The Sikarwar Rajputs ruled at nearby Bayana and the Tomars built the fortress of Gwalior in the hilly terrain of the Vindhyan Ranges. One arm of this range of low hills slices through Sikri. To the north-west stretch the deserts of Rajasthan, to the east is the expanse of the Indo-Gangetic plains, to the south are the ravines of Chambal and beyond it is the Deccan Plateau. For an empire builder like Akbar the strategic location of Agra and Fatehpur Sikri made them ideal for a capital city.

In the twelfth century, Muhammad of Ghor occupied Delhi and soon captured Bayana and the region became a part of the kingdom of the sultans of Delhi. There are mosques here built during the Sultanate years and in the Shahi Masjid in Shaikhon ka Mohalla there is an inscription dated 1314 saying the mosque was built during the reign of Allauddin Khalji. Gwalior was still being ruled by the Tomars

► *Over the centuries Sikri has seen the rise and fall of kingdoms, as the pilgrims have come to a Sufi shrine.*

so the Bayana-Sikri region was the southern border of the Sultanate kingdoms. Bayana lost its premier position when in 1502 Sikander Lodi began to build a new capital at Agra. Then in 1526 his son Ibrahim Lodi was defeated by Zahiruddin Muhammad Babur at Panipat and the Mughals appeared centre stage and grabbed the attention of the world for the next three centuries.

Babur is described by Louise Nicholson as 'poet, diarist, soldier, statesman and adventurer' and he set the tone of the dynasty with his blend of ruthless conquest and a love of architecture and culture. The Mughals were not just warriors, they were also aesthetes and patrons of all the arts. Babur chose Agra instead of Delhi as his capital and it was here that he faced the greatest military challenge from the Rajputs when a confederacy led by Rana Sangram Singh of Mewar made a last stand at Khanwa a few miles from Sikri. Babur triumphed and in his autobiography *Baburnama* he mentions visiting Sikri on his way to battle and then on his way back after his victory and this is when he renamed the place as 'Shukri' or thanksgiving. He writes that he laid out a garden with Jal Mahal, a lake palace, and a baoli, a step well in celebration of his triumph but both have disappeared.

From the Hindu *Saik* and *Sekrikya* to Babur's heartfelt Shukri and then Akbar's Fatehabad and

▼ *Mustard fields along the road to Sikri.*

▼ *Kos minars were Mughal milestones.*

Fatehpur, the site would carry many names but it would be Akbar who would put it on the map of travellers. One day the top of the hill would be covered by palaces, pavilions, aqueducts, a mosque, walls, gateways and the mausoleum of the saint he revered. What he created was more an administrative and cultural centre than a citadel. He would start building it in 1571 and live there for fourteen years and then in 1585 inexplicably ride away, never to return. The reason for his abandoning Fatehpur Sikri has intrigued historians for centuries and there are many hotly debated theories but no convincing answers. Only Akbar knew why he never came back and he took the reasons with him.

Look up the Hill

The first glimpse of Fatehpur Sikri is of a hill topped with the reddish brown crenellated walls and battlements of a medieval city. As the car moves up the steep slope there are the ruined kiosks of a bazaar on both sides of the road and you will enter through the gateway called Agra Gate. Beyond it lies Akbar's personal and at times idiosyncratic world—his city of victory and also his fortress of dreams. For travellers this has been their first sight of Fatehpur Sikri and they came by the hundred, traders and adventurers, royal envoys, soldiers and philosophers, painters and musicians, coming to the court of one of the richest

▼ *A view of the Sikri village today.*

▼ *Walls and gateways of the city.*

'The breadth of the city is by no means so great as the length, because everyone has tried to be close to the river bank, and consequently the water front is occupied by the costly palaces of all the famous lords which makes it appear very gay and magnificent and extends for a distance of six kos.'

***Francisco Pelsaert**, a Dutch traveller who visited India in 1629 describing the city of Fatehpur Sikri.*

kings in the world, the legendary Grand Mughal, and their writings bring us a contemporary view of the city and rare glimpses of the life of not just royalty and nobility but also of the ordinary people.

During Akbar's reign Ralph Fitch arrived from England in 1583, the Venetian jeweller Cesare Federici in 1565 and the Jesuit priest Rudolfo Acquaviva in 1578 came from Italy and two Spanish Jesuits, Antonio Monserrate in 1580 and Edoardo Barbosa in 1560. The appearance of the Jesuits was a result of news travelling to Europe of Akbar's eclectic curiosity about all religions and the Jesuits came hurrying to India hoping to convert the Mughal monarch. Their writings give us invaluable details of life in Akbar's court, especially the memoirs of Monserrate who spent many years in the royal court and saw him up close. As Ralph Fitch, one of the earliest English visitors, writes, clearly impressed by

◄ *Akbari Mahal. Akbar first used red sandstone embellished with carvings on the palaces within Agra Fort.*

what he saw of Agra and Fatehpur Sikri, 'they were two very great cities, either of them much greater than London and very populous'.

The first impression of the royal enclosure will be of the sun's rays sparking off the red sandstone walls of the palaces. The building material was easy to find, it is the stone of the ridge itself and it is a colour that is hard to capture in words, a shade of ochre red that at times has a touch of pink and in the shadows turns a shade of maroon. On this wherever a highlight has been inlaid in marble it gleams and sparkles creating a red-gold ambience. It is then easy to imagine Akbar's stocky, energetic figure walking swiftly from the Diwan-i-Aam to the offices of the Daftar Khana followed by his nobles; the clatter of horses' hooves at the gate; the call of guards as they clashed their spears and a peacock perched on the roof of a pavilion.

There is much to discover here and one can spend days finding hidden wonders in rubble-strewn corners but the best are around three main areas. First the public space of the first courtyard with the Diwan-i-Aam, the Hall of Public Audience, the Diwan-i-Khas, the Hall of Private Audience; the Panch Mahal and the pavilion that the travel guides rather fancifully call Ankh Michauli. The next courtyard leads to Akbar's private world with the square lotus pool called Anup Talao placed before his personal palace the Khwabgah and the pavilion called the Turkish Sultana's Palace. Then the many palaces

▶ *View of the main courtyard from the Anup Talao with the Diwan-i-Khas in the centre.*

▲ *Panch Mahal. Medieval palaces often had a tower to enjoy the cool summer breeze.*

of the haramsara or seraglio–Jodh Bai's Palace, Sunahra Makan, Hawa Mahal and Birbal's Palace. A short walk away is the spiritual heart of the city, the main congregational mosque, the Jami Masjid with the towering gateway, the Buland Darwaza at one end and the marble mausoleum of Sheikh Salim Chishti placed in the middle of the expanse of the courtyard like a bejewelled casket. Exploring all these monuments will take you a day.

Contemporary writings are of little help in identifying the palaces and many were never named, so the names of many of them were the inventions of nineteenth-century guides who were taking around European visitors and somehow the names have stuck. Historians have protested at a pavilion in the public

▲ *Ruins of the caravanserai that once stood near the Agra Gate.*

area being called Ankh Michauli where according to garrulous guides Akbar played blind-man's-buff with his queens! First of all queens would not come into this area and then Akbar, a busy and rather majestic king who created an elaborate and ceremonial court culture, was not the sort to be silly and playful. Then there is a huge, intricately carved pavilion that some long forgotten guide dubbed as Queen Jodh Bai's kitchen or the palace they called Samosa Bhawan because its triangular roof reminded them of the fried savoury you find in Agra's food shops.

As historians have not been able to find conclusive identification in contemporary writing, the popular names, however incongruous, remained and will be used in this book. Information about

◀ *Jodh Bai's Palace. The main entrance was guarded by Rajput soldiers.*

Fatehpur Sikri can be found in the royal chronicles of Akbar's official historian Abul Fazl, in the volumes of the *Akbarnama* and *Ain-i-Akbari* and the private and more critical chronicle, Badauni's *Muntakhab al-Tawarikh*. Akbar's son Jahangir who spent his childhood here writes in his autobiography *Tuzuk-i-Jahangiri*, 'that hill, full of wild beasts, became a city containing all kinds of gardens and buildings'. Then there are the writings of travellers and a visual record

in the miniature paintings produced in the ateliers of the city. Some buildings mentioned in these texts cannot be identified, the most famous being the Ibadat Khana, Akbar's House of Worship and religious debate or the Imperial Library where he is said to have collected 20,000 books.

Today Fatehpur Sikri is a UNESCO World Heritage Site; tourists and local sightseers blend in with the pilgrims who come to pray at the Dargah of the

▼ *Ruins of the many outer buildings that surround the palaces.*

Sufi saint. For a long a time the royal enclosure was forgotten by the world and the rest of the city gradually vanished but the spiritual centre was never forgotten, it was always alive as the pilgrims never abandoned the place. As a matter of fact when the ghostly city lay silent, the descendants of Sheikh Salim Chishti maintained the palaces and saved them from ruin.

Abul Fazl, royal historian and friend of Akbar wrote of his king's plans for a city, 'Fatehpur was a village ... situated twelve kos distant from Agra ... it rose to be a city of the first importance. A masonry fort was erected and two elephants carved in stone at its gate inspired astonishment ... by command of His Majesty a mosque, a college and a religious house were also built upon the hill, the like of which few travellers can name ... in the vicinity is a quarry of red stone whence columns and slabs of any dimension can be excavated ... under his Majesty's patronage carpets and fine stuff are woven and numerous craftsmen have full occupation.'

A childless king, a Sufi saint and a Rajput princess brought us this extraordinary city on a hill. The capital of an empire, a courtly and enlightened centre of culture and crafts and the city of a king's imagination, Fatehpur Sikri is an unforgettable experience.

◀ *Through the centuries the pilgrims have never stopped coming to the dargah of Salim Chishti.*

BEGINNING OF THE EMPIRE

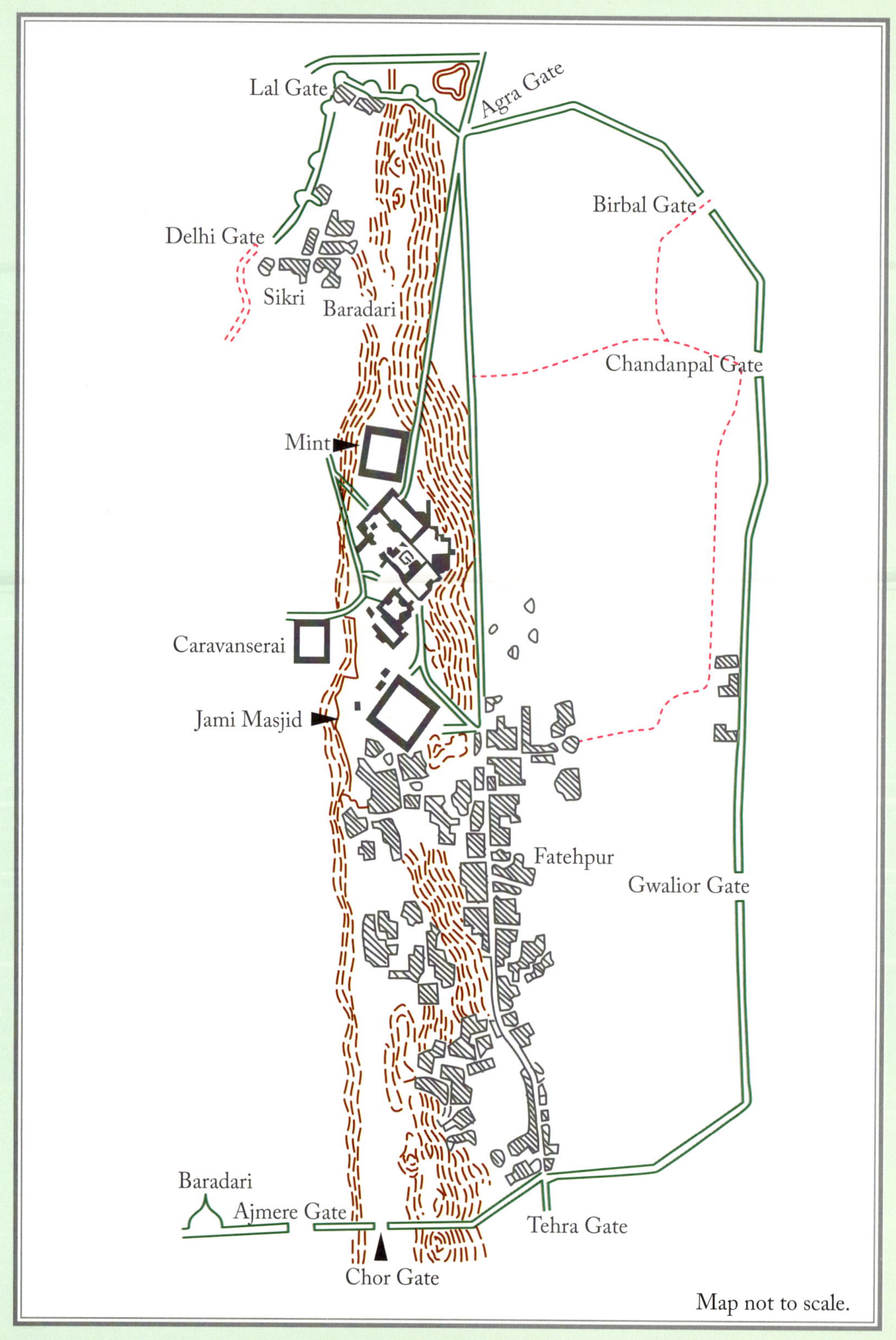
Lal Gate
Agra Gate
Birbal Gate
Delhi Gate
Sikri
Baradari
Chandanpal Gate
Mint
Caravanserai
Jami Masjid
Fatehpur
Gwalior Gate
Baradari
Ajmere Gate
Tehra Gate
Chor Gate
Map not to scale.

Beginning of the empire

'Babur made arrangements for Ibrahim, as a mark of respect to be buried where he fell and his tomb still stands as Panipat. But it was typical of Babur that to celebrate his own victory he created at Panipat not another monument but a pleasant garden.'

-Bamber Gascoigne

The world calls them the Mughals but within the family they preferred the title Taimuriya or Timurids. The founder of the dynasty, Zahiruddin Babur may have been the king of a small kingdom in Central Asia but he traced his lineage to two famous conquerors. On his mother's side he descended from the Mongol Chinghiz Khan and from his father's from the Chaghatai Turk, Timur who built an empire in Persia. For the Mughals, somehow the connection to the cosmopolitan Timur, instead of the nomadic and barbaric Mongols, was more valuable. Timur was no less violent but he also built a fabulous city like Samarkand, filling it with palaces and mosques and became a patron of poets, philosophers and artists and in their palaces the Mughals tried to replicate the cultured image of the Persian court. The barbaric nomadic style of Chinghiz did not match their image of being benign and civilized despots. As historian Bamber Gascoigne commented, 'Babur would ... have been horrified to discover that the dynasty founded by him in India would become known throughout the world as Moghul—an adaptation of Mughul, the Persian word for Mongol.'

◀ *The plan of the fortified settlement of Fatehpur Sikri showing the Royal Citadel on the hilltop.*

The empire was really built by the third king of the dynasty, Akbar, but its foundations were laid by his grandfather Babur. They had much in common both in character and in the way the fates treated them. Most intriguingly, they both faced the most crucial juncture in their reigns at the same battlefield in Panipat. The difference was that at the first battle the grandfather was a forty-three year old veteran warrior and ruler and at the second, the grandson a fourteen year old prince. Babur remained a big influence in Akbar's life and he used to listen to readings from his grandfather's autobiography, the *Baburnama* often. It was these two men who set the tone of the Mughal Empire, not just as empire builders but also in their religious tolerance, eclectic cultural interests and administrative skills. To understand Akbar and his impulse to create a city like Fatehpur Sikri we have to first know Babur's story.

Babur (1526–1530)

Reflecting his name that means tiger, Babur was a reckless adventurer and a ruthless conqueror but intriguingly he had the soul of an artist, loved nature, composed poetry and kept a diary. In his journal the *Baburnama* he gives us a first hand account of a life filled with the most improbable ups and downs where one day he is a penniless nomad and the next day a king. He was born in 1483 in the royal family of Ferghana, which is located in today's Uzbekistan, and

▶ *Winter falls over Babur's modest tomb in Kabul, set within a charbagh garden.*

conscious of his imperial lineage he was an ambitious prince with grandiose plans of conquest.

Babur idolised Timur and his dream was to capture Timur's legendary capital city, Samarkand. The problem was that there were many claimants to Timur's throne and he won and lost the city a number of times and in the bargain lost Ferghana too. He wandered around Afghanistan like a common nomad with his raggedy band of comrades, barely surviving by raiding forts and villages in what he called his 'throneless times' until he managed to capture Kabul. It was as the king of Kabul that he stopped hankering for Samarkand, looked east instead and saw a land known for its fabulous wealth—India. India had tempted soldiers of fortune for centuries. It began with Alexander, and had long been on the itinerary of invaders like Mongols, Turks, Persians, Huns and Afghans. Babur's ancestor Timur had gone as far as Delhi and come away with a fabulous booty. So when he turned his covetous eyes towards Hindustan, Babur was following many others before him including his hero Timur. Only with Babur there was one crucial difference—his opponents would be Muslims and not Hindus, because for the past four centuries North India had been ruled by successive dynasties of Sultans from their capital in Delhi.

▼ Babur's Tomb. While in India Babur had dreamed of going back to Kabul.

▼ Babur's Tomb. All the Mughal kings lie in graves covered in marble.

Babur gathered his forces against the Afghan Sultan Ibrahim Lodi, a king so unpopular that his nobles were willing to help Babur. The two armies met on 20 April 1526 in an open area near the town of Panipat and at first sight it did not look very favourable as Ibrahim had massed one lakh soldiers and a thousand elephants that stood swaying like a wall before them. Babur's army was a quarter of that in size, of just 25,000 men and horses but no elephants. The one crucial advantage that he had was his artillery with a regiment of Persian gunners firing matchlocks and another was his superior battle strategy.

At the First Battle of Panipat Babur won himself an Indian kingdom and exactly thirty years later his grandson Akbar would return to the same battlefield to claim his inheritance.

Unlike Timur, Babur intended to stay in India. He established his capital at Agra from where he planned to carry on his plans of conquest. His toughest challenge came the following year from a confederacy of Rajput kingdoms led by Rana Sangram Singh of Mewar. The two armies met at Khanwa, just beyond Sikri and the Rajputs put up a fierce fight but were defeated as the Mughal artillery again played a crucial role. In his journal Babur commented rather cynically that the Rajputs knew how to fight but not how to win. Then tragedy struck when in 1530, just four years after conquering Hindustan, Babur died at the age of forty-seven.

In many ways, Babur and later his grandson Akbar

▼ *Babur's Tomb. The interiors are decorated with an inlay of coloured tiles.*

established the traditions of the Mughal dynasty. It was led by men who were not just warriors and rulers but also treasured books, patronised painters and singers and in most cases headed royal establishments that were based on a relaxed attitude to religion and an enlightened spirit of tolerance. At Akbar's court in Fatehpur Sikri what was prized was talent and appointments were made according to ability and not religion.

Similarly, Fatehpur Sikri encapsulates not just the spirit of Akbar but also that of his father and grandfather. Babur began the family tradition of architecture, though he was more interested in building open pavilions set within formal gardens. May be if he had lived longer he would have built a city like his grandson. Both he and Humayun passionately loved books and during the years when they lost their kingdoms and wandered homeless they still carried their precious manuscripts with them, loaded on the back of camels. The dreamy Humayun even took his favourite books with him when he set out to war. The women in the family were often erudite women, like Babur's daughter Gulbadan Begum who wrote her memoirs, titled *Humayunama*. Later Akbar would build a huge library at Fatehpur Sikri said to have 20,000 books and he got Hindu epics like the *Mahabharata* translated into Persian. Babur and then Humayun patronised painters and one day Akbar would establish a *karkhana* or atelier for miniature painters in Fatehpur Sikri.

Babur in Sikri

It was Babur who came to Sikri and he also built here. He first saw Sikri on his way to the battle at Khanwa, stopped and surveyed the terrain and wrote, 'It crossed my mind that the well-watered ground for a large camp was at Sikri.' It was a pleasant place where a lake had been created by damming a stream and Babur with his poet's eye was enchanted by the landscape and the birds and trees around him. On his way back to Agra after his victory he rested here for two days and supervised the creation of a garden and a Jal Mahal, a water pavilion, though both have disappeared. By a well that must have stood within the long vanished garden there is an inscription, 'At the command of Zahir-ud-din Muhammad Babur, Badshah Ghazi, may God perpetuate his realm and rule. The construction of this well was, through the Divine grace, completed in the year AH 933 (1527) after (he) had returned conquering and victorious from his campaign against the misbelieving Rana Sanga.' He called the place *shukri* or thanksgiving and clearly had a good time. A man who enjoyed his wine and an opiate called *majun*, he writes with his typical candour that on a trip on the lake, 'We went over by boat, had an awning set up on it and elected for *majun*.'

Babur was an amazing mix of a ruthless warrior, a poet and a naturalist and all through his life kept a journal where he described the land and the people, the flora and fauna of the places he visited. According to his daughter Gulbadan, he came to Sikri to spend time organising his notes and writing down

▲ *A panoramic view of the impressive ramparts and gateways of Fatehpur Sikri.*

his impressions of India. The book is not just about his military exploits but the section on India is full of fascinating details of the social customs of the people, the fruits and flowers, the animals and the birds of the land and as Gascoigne notes with amusement, 'the want of good manners, decent trousers and cool streams' in India.

Gulbadan who was then six years old remembers her father busy with his papers in his garden at Sikri and Babur himself writes about the time when a sudden storm scattered his precious notes and then as the tent collapsed, 'the books were drenched under water and gathered together with much difficulty. We laid them in the fold of a woollen throne-carpet, put this on the throne and on it piled blankets', then a fire was lit and he was 'busy ... drying folios and sections.'

Humayun (1530–1556)

Babur was succeeded by his eldest son Humayun and what he had fought so hard to achieve was nearly lost by his feckless successor. A superstitious, sentimental, impulsive man who was more interested in astrology, wine, opium and poetry he lacked the ruthlessness that was needed to hold the kingdom together. Humayun was brave and could win battles but he was not very good at consolidating his victories. As Gascoigne says about him, 'there could hardly have been a character less suited to the arduous task of retaining the family's new possessions.' The kingdom was in its infancy, the provinces full of rebellious Afghan noblemen who had to be subdued and he couldn't even control his three recalcitrant brothers Kamran, Askari and Hindal who were constantly trying to dethrone him.

◀ *Humayun's Tomb. The design of a tomb set in a garden became the template for all Mughal mausoleums.*

▼ *Humayun's Tomb. A variety of marble inlay highlights were used around the arches and screens.*

Humayun was defeated by the Afghan Sher Shah Sur and it looked like Babur's dream of an Indian kingdom was over. Hindustan was lost to Humayun and his brothers now gleefully divided up the rest of Babur's empire and chased him all across Punjab. It was during these years of wandering that he took shelter with the Hindu Raja of Umarkot. Here on 15 October 1542 his wife Hamida Bano Begum gave birth to his first son, who was named Jalaluddin Muhammad Akbar. As the historian Haider wrote of his birth, he was 'the child of a Sunni father and a Shia mother born in Hindustan in the land of Sufism at the house of a Hindu.' It was the perfect lineage for a Mughal king.

Humayun finally found support from Shah Tahmasp, the ruler of Persia who financed an army. His fortunes turned as he defeated Kamran who was ruling at Kabul and reclaimed his Afghan kingdom. Meanwhile the Sur kingdom had collapsed at the death of Sher Shah's son Islam Shah and in 1555 the Mughal general Bairam Khan defeated the Afghan forces. Humayun returned to India and his wife Hamida, sister Gulbadan and son Akbar soon joined him.

After that he ran out of luck again and this time permanently. Sher Shah had built palaces inside Din Panah which the royal family had occupied and Humayun had turned the octagonal tower called Sher Mandal into a library. One day in 1556, as he was coming down the steep flight of steps he heard the cry of the muezzin calling the faithful to prayer and as he hurried down, the edge of his long coat caught under his foot and he tumbled to his death.

After defeating Humayun, Sher Shah Sur occupied his citadel Din Panah. Here he built a double storeyed octagonal tower called Sher Mandal. When Humayun once again occupied the citadel he turned it into a library. In 1556, he died when he tripped and fell down its stairs.

Akbar at Panipat

At that time a thirteen year old Akbar was with Bairam Khan, fighting rebels in the Punjab. Bairam immediately crowned him king in a hurried coronation held in a garden at a place called Kalanaur. The boy king wore a golden robe and a tiara, and sat on a stone platform and 450 years later, this platform still stands amidst the wheat fields near Gurdaspur in Punjab. Akbar may have been crowned king but his kingdom stood on very shaky foundations. Fortunately Humayun had appointed Bairam Khan as Akbar's guardian and the wise advice of this loyal old soldier saved the Mughal kingdom from collapsing for the second time.

Akbar's toughest challenge came from an unexpected source, not from an Afghan nobleman but a Hindu commoner. His name was Hemchandra and people called him Hemu and he began his life as a small time trader in Rewari and somehow rose to become the chief minister of one of the Afghan claimants to the Sur throne, Adil Shah Sur. Hemu was a short, frail man who had never been a soldier but he possessed a brilliant military mind and became a courageous general who never lost a battle. In 1556, while Akbar and Bairam Khan were away in Punjab, Hemu suddenly swept in and captured Agra and Delhi. He immediately abandoned his master and declared himself king, taking the title of Vikramaditya.

Akbar and Bairam Khan now had to take a hard decision. The picture did not look good, their army was small and after years of fighting the men were tired. Hemu had a much larger army, he had won twenty battles in a row and was in possession of Delhi. Akbar still had his Afghan territories and many of his advisers felt he should retreat to Kabul, build a new army and come back to fight another day. The harder and more foolhardy option was to stand and face the enemy immediately and for the first time the teenaged king showed the steel in his character and decided to stay and fight. Just like Babur before him, he was gambling his kingdom on the result of one battle.

Once again a Mughal marched to the fields of Panipat and once again his small army looked unequal to the fight. Hemu had 50,000 Afghan and Rajput soldiers and 1,500 elephants while Akbar and Bairam Khan were leading 25,000 battle weary men and a few horses. The two armies met on 5 November 1556 and it was a lucky accident that gave Akbar his victory. Hemu led his army into battle seated on his famous fighting elephant Hawai. His initial charge was so fierce it threw the Mughals into confusion and then a ferocious battle began and after a while it began to look as if Hemu was winning. Just then a stray arrow hit Hemu in the eye and he slumped unconscious in his howdah and thinking that he was dead, his men wavered and then fled the battlefield. Hemu was captured, brought before Akbar and beheaded and the Mughals returned to Delhi in triumph.

Family Tree of the Mughals

Babur traced his ancestry to two conquerors—the Mongol Chinghiz Khan and the Chaghatai Turk, Timur who ruled Persia. The Mughal dynasty was very proud of its Persian connections and introduced Persian traditions in art, architecture and court etiquette. They called themselves Timuriya after the Persian king and would not have approved of being called Mughal after the barbaric Mongols. The dynasty would rule from 1526 to 1857 and at its zenith the empire covered most of the Indian subcontinent.

The Mughal Empire lasted from 1526 to 1857 when the last Mughal king, Bahadur Shah II was dethroned by the British and banished to Rangoon, Burma. It is the first six kings—Babur, Humayun, Akbar, Jahangir, Shah Jahan and Aurangzeb who ruled over a true empire that covered most of the Indian subcontinent and parts of Afghanistan. The decline begins from the death of Aurangzeb in 1707. Sadly by the end, the empire built by Akbar, had been reduced to just the area around their capital Delhi.

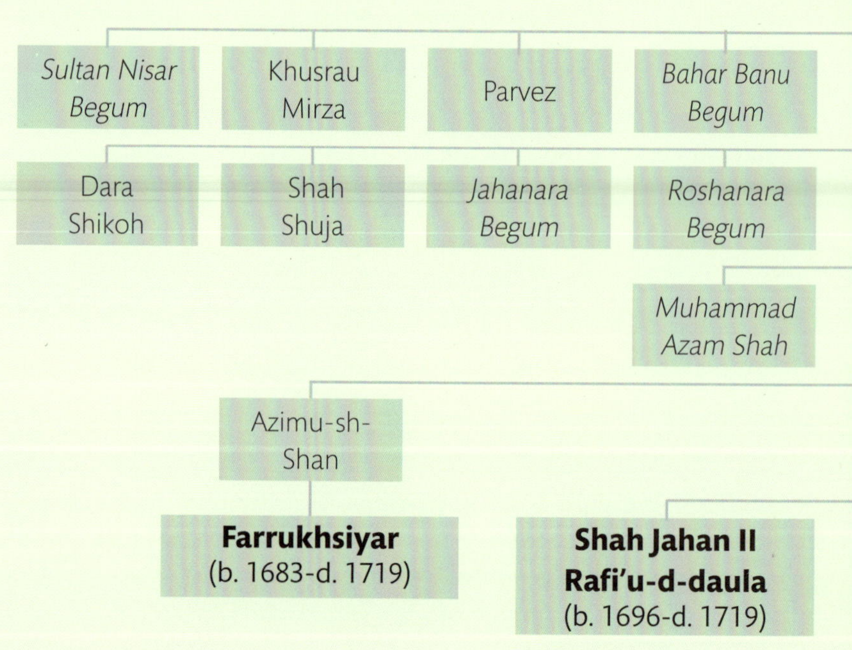

Babur
(b. 1483-d. 1531)
Humayun
(b. 1508-d. 1556)
Askari Mirza
Hindal Mirza
Gulrukh Begum
Kamran Mirza
Akbar
(b. 1542-d. 1605)
Muhammad Hakim
Jahangir
(b. 1569-d. 1627)
Khanzada Khanim
Shah Murad
Daniyal
Shakarunnisa Begum
Aram Banu Begum
Shah Jahan
(b. 1592-d. 1666)
Shahrayar
Jahandar
Aurangzeb
(b. 1618-d. 1707)
Murad Baksh
Bahadur Shah I
(b. 1643 d. 1712)
Muhammad Akbar
Muhammad Kam Baksh
Rafi'u-sh-shan
Jahandar Shah
(b. 1664-d. 1713)
Khujista Akhtar
Nekosiyar
Muhayyiu-s-sana
Rafi'u-d-Darjat
(b. 1699-d. 1719)
Muhammad Ibrahim
Muhammad Shah
(b1702-d. 1748)
Shah Jahan III
Alamgir II
(b. 1699-d. 1759)
Ahmad Shah Bahadur
(b. 1725-d. 1754)
Shah Alam II
(b. 1728-d. 1806)
Bedar Bakht
Akbar Shah II
(b. 1760-d. 1837)
Bahadur Shah Zafar
(b. 1775 d. 1862)

Influential Women

In the writing of western travellers it was called the harem or seraglio, the Mughals called it the haramsara, zenana or simply mahal. It was the innermost and most guarded area of a fortress where the royal women—queens, princesses, female relatives and concubines lived in luxury surrounded by maids and eunuchs. In Fatehpur Sikri the haramsara was placed next to Akbar's personal palace the Khwabgah, across a courtyard and connected by covered corridors. The women were in the strictest purdah, living as historian Abraham Eraly calls it, in a 'vacuum-sealed world of their own'. However the popular image of languorous women living in the lap of luxury was not always true, especially for the women belonging to the royal family. They were scholars and businesswomen, using their earnings for charity and being energetically involved in politics. Of course their power emanated from their closeness to the king and was usually limited to the women of the immediate family—mother, aunts, wives, sisters and daughters.

Right from the time of Babur the history of the Mughals is interwoven with stories of powerful royal women playing an active part in politics. Babur was just twelve when his father died and other relatives claimed the throne. If he survived it was because of his formidable grandmother Ehsan Daulat Begum who gathered loyal noblemen to her side and marched out with an army in his support. Similarly Babur's sister Khanzada played a pivotal role during her nephew Humayun's troubles with his three brothers. Akbar, born in the middle of a vicious fratricidal war and often separated from his nomadic parents survived the turmoil, was taken care of by the royal women.

After the tumultuous years of Babur and Humayun, during Akbar's reign these women led a much more settled existence and at Fatehpur Sikri he gave them large airy palaces, courtyards, hammams for their baths and gardens for relaxation. Being an instinctive organiser

▲ *Minor Haramsara. The two rows of rooms are near the main harem palaces and minor queens, princesses and concubines lived here.*

he also gave the haramsara a hierarchy and administrative system and it was always headed by a member of the king's immediate family. He appointed his mother Hamida Bano Begum as the head of the harem, his grandson Shah Jahan, at the death of his wife Mumtaz, appointed his daughter Jahanara who was just seventeen. This was not an easy job as it involved running an establishment of hundreds of royal women, maids and children. Akbar is said to have married a few hundred women and had many concubines. Hamida Bano also held the royal seal, called the uzuk, which was an engraved signet ring. All important royal decrees had to be stamped with it and

that meant she also read them and could advice the king.

In Akbar's life the most influential women were his mother Hamida, aunt Gulbadan and three of his many wives Ruquaiya Begum, Salima Sultan and Mariam-us-Zamani, the Hindu princess of Amber who was the mother of the heir, Prince Salim. Also for a few early years there was his foster mother Maham Anaga. Their seclusion did not mean these women were unaware of the latest happenings in the empire as they regularly attended the royal audiences, sitting behind a screen and unseen by

◀ *Jodh Bai's Palace. These small covered balconies were called jharokhas.*

▲ *Jodh Bai's Palace. The northern and southern wings have roofs tiled in bright turquoise, adding a feminine touch to the complex.*

others they heard and saw everything. At the royal court they heard the governors and ministers give their reports to the king, heard petitions by the nobility and common citizens and watched Akbar pass judgement in criminal cases and they were familiar with all the important men of the court. There are reports of them interceding on behalf of people when they met the king in the harem or even calling out for mercy for someone from behind the screen.

As the harem was the best guarded area in the palace, the king felt safe there. Akbar would spend many hours here working, conferring privately with ministers and getting reports from spies and the women were often nearby, listening, advising and criticising. Akbar was too strong a personality and too imperious a king to allow these women any real power but he treated them with love and courtesy and did listen to them. This was very different from Jahangir who let his queen Nurjahan virtually run the empire and grandson Shah Jahan who was actively advised by his queen Mumtaz Mahal. For Akbar, the women were a part of his team of trusted advisers,

especially in matters of the family but he was the final authority and the unquestioned ruler.

The family had a tradition of treating their women with respect; the king met the senior women regularly and would even come out of the city to greet them when they returned from their travels. In a large clan forever in turmoil because of the ambitions of their men, the women often had to play peacemaker. The empire was the family business and these supremely pragmatic women understood their role as the guardians of peace and amity. Khanzada went back and forth between Humayun and his troublesome brothers and when Salim rebelled against Akbar it was Hamida Bano and Gulbadan who had to convince him to come back to court and beg for his father's forgiveness. Hamida is said to have pushed her grandson so that the prince fell at Akbar's feet.

These women also proved that even if you were behind the veil it did not mean you withdrew from the world. They all received generous allowances and part of that was in the form of land, a jagir from where they earned rent. Many even ran businesses and Hamida and Mariam-us-Zamani owned trading ships that plied in the Arabian Sea. They ran all their business enterprises with the help of managers whom they met sitting behind a screen and scrutinised all accounts and even passed royal orders. Many of these orders, *firman* signed by them have survived. They used their large incomes for gifts, lavish entertainments and charity. The marriages of the Mughal children were arranged by them and there are reports of gigantic and splendid celebrations all organised and paid for by a queen or princess.

Of course all the royal women were not loyal to the king and they took sides when the princes battled for the throne. The most famous case is of the two daughters of Akbar's grandson Shah Jahan—Jahanara and Roshanara. The first supported Dara Shikoh who lost the fight

◄ *A typical Hindu sculptural motif of a vase, vines and flowers.*

and the latter Aurangzeb who captured the throne. Shah Jahan who was still alive at the time was banished to Agra and Jahanara joined him there while Roshanara took over Jahanara's position as the head of the haramsara and also took on her official title of Begum Sahib. Akbar himself faced the wrath of his stepmother Mah Chuchak Begum who was the mother of his only brother Mirza Hakim. At Humayun's death Hakim was made the governor of Kabul but his mother often encouraged him to rebel and the province remained a source of perpetual trouble as Mah Chuchak interfered in everything. Finally a furious Akbar was forced to march out with his army and sort things out.

What is remarkable for the time is how many of these women were also scholars and poets. At Akbar's request Gulbadan wrote her brother's biography titled *Humayunama* which is surprisingly well written. Ruqaiya Begum is said to have had a large library and Jahanara and Aurangzeb's daughter Zinat-un-nisa were popular poets. They may have spent their lives behind what Abul Fazl described as the 'screen of purity' but they asserted themselves with courage and sagacity and became women of real substance.

▶ *Details of a doorway in the Haramsara with the Hindu influence reflected in the torans.*

THE JEWEL OF THE EMPIRE

The jewel of the empire

'He was more humane and more generous than most men of his time and more tolerant. Above all, he possessed creative imagination which can use success to transform a situation rather than humiliate an opponent and can use the ordinary motive of the average man for constructive purposes.'

-Percival Spear

It was not going to be easy for a boy king. Akbar could not have kept the kingdom safe on his own and if it survived it was because of the loyalty and ability of one man, Bairam Khan. For the first four years Akbar remained a sort of apprentice king, managed by his regent and the harem matrons and as his historian Abul Fazl put it rather delicately, he was a king 'behind the veil'. First the old general defeated the rebellious Afghans who were running about the countryside fomenting trouble and then he ran the government with firm efficiency. To his credit he did not take advantage of the vulnerable young king and seize the throne himself.

Then as the boy matured into a strong willed young man conflict became inevitable. Bairam Khan was a domineering man with a harsh temper who favoured a coterie of favourites and that made him unpopular. His hold on governance was so relentless that Akbar began to get impatient as he was not allowed any say in the matters of state. Surprisingly the opposition began in the harem with the active encouragement of queen mother Hamida Bano and led by Akbar's shrewd and ambitious foster mother

◀ *Buland Darwaza. The massive bulk of the gateway was lightened by the use of marble decorations.*

Maham Anaga who wanted her son Adham Khan to replace Bairam Khan. The dismissal was done in the usual Mughal style, with subtle firmness. Akbar went to Delhi from where he sent a courteous letter to his regent in Agra saying that as the old man had been working too hard and he deserved a holiday, and the king would finance a pilgrimage to Mecca. Bairam once again displayed exemplary loyalty and obeyed. Matters would have ended gracefully but for the tactless Maham Anaga who sent an army after Bairam to make sure he really did leave. This was too much for the old retainer who turned back to fight. Bairam lost, was captured and brought before Akbar who had by then realised his mistake. No one knew more than him just how much he owed to his regent and the two men were reconciled. Akbar treated his mentor with honour and Bairam once again left for Mecca but sadly he never made it to his destination. He was assassinated in Gujarat by an Afghan soldier who bore him a personal grudge.

The influence of Maham Anaga did not last too long either, mainly because of her headstrong son Adham Khan. They made the mistake of thinking that they could control the king the way Bairam Khan had done, forgetting that Akbar was now eighteen. Adham's early acts of disobedience were provocation enough, and he was forgiven only because of Akbar's respect for his mother. His most serious transgression was when he tried to keep back the booty after the conquest of Malwa instead of sending it all to Agra. Akbar had to march out and reprimand him and as a consequence another man, Atkah Khan, was made prime minister. Finally, Adham went too far and murdered Atkah Khan, right outside Akbar's bed chamber. Hearing the commotion Akbar came out and punched Adham so hard he fell unconscious and showing no mercy Akbar ordered his foster brother to be thrown off the walls of the fort. Then he went to the harem and informed Maham Anaga of his decision, she accepted it and died soon after. This interregnum of harem rule had only lasted eighteen months and Akbar was now in complete control.

▶ *Agra Fort. The forbidding outer walls with a moat, ramparts and battlements.*

A Mughal Monarch

In many ways he was different from the earlier Muslim rulers and the most significant was the way he viewed his kingdom and his subjects - not as their occupier and conqueror but as their king. By the sixteenth century, North India had been ruled by Muslim sultans for four centuries and it had led to a great social divide between the ruling nobility, mainly made up of Afghans, Persians and Turks, and their subjects who were mostly Hindus. The discrimination was clearly dictated by religion. Hindus could not rise to high posts in the government or the army, no Hindu could be a member of the nobility and religious taxes like *jiziya* was deeply resented. Sultans took pride in their title of ghazi or defender of the faith and destroyed temples, burnt holy books and encouraged conversions. So for the general populace the sultans remained foreign occupiers and were never accepted as one of their own.

Akbar was shrewd enough to realise that if he wanted to rule in peace he had to gain the loyalty of all his subjects. The challenge was to

change his image from a hated conqueror to the popular king and that meant he had to be accepted by the Hindus. This was a revolutionary change of attitude at a time when religious bigotry was the accepted norm. A policy of religious tolerance was truly extraordinary and it reflected both his imperialistic ambitions and his unusual character. At one level, his decision was pragmatic and a part of a strategy to extend his kingdom because the empire always came first for Akbar. At the other, there was no artifice in his reaching out to his subjects, he was a genuinely liberal and open minded man who exhibited a deeply felt curiosity about other religions. For a medieval monarch his enlightened attitude towards his subjects and their religion made him a very unusual king and both these elements will be reflected in the way he would plan and build Fatehpur Sikri. And if the heart of his city was the tomb of a Sufi saint who was revered by people of both religions it was because for Akbar the guiding spirit of his reign was acceptance and tolerance.

▲ *Jami Masjid. The expanse of the mosque courtyard with Salim Chishti's tomb in the centre.*

Akbar's first tactical decision was abolishing the hated *jiziya* tax and this simple gesture sent the message that to him all his subjects were equal. Another intelligent move was when he was twenty, he decided to marry a Rajput princess, the daughter of Bihari Mal, the Raja of Amber and soon other Rajput princesses followed her into the haramsara. The marriage alliance itself was not unusual as Hindu princesses had married sultans before but they were always forced to convert to Islam. Akbar allowed them to practise their religion freely. At Fatehpur Sikri he built a separate palace for the Hindu queens with their own temples and kitchens and they celebrated Hindu festivals at court with the king happily joining in. In this way he disarmed the biggest threat to his kingdom which came from the Rajput kings. He welcomed marriage alliances with all the Rajput clans and gave the kings sovereignty within their kingdoms but the ones who refused his offer, like Chittor, were ruthlessly conquered. Next he appointed

▲ *Entrance of Jodh Bai's Palace. In contemporary chronicles it was called Shabistan-i-Iqbal.*

Hindus to senior posts in the government and army, Rajputs were appointed generals and they were given titles as noblemen and became the fighting arm of his army. The story of Akbar's rule is also the story of these Rajput clans and their contributions to the creation of the Mughal Empire and at Fatehpur Sikri men like Man Singh, Todar Mal and Birbal, all rajas, built their mansions near the king. In Akbar's government people rose according to their ability and this created an organisation that was innovative, efficient and deeply loyal to the king.

There was a strong presence of Rajput noblemen in the Mughal court till the end of the dynasty and it all began with Akbar.

A Hunger for Land

Who really laid the foundation of the Mughal Empire, Babur or Akbar? According to historian Percival Spear, 'Babur was the founder only in the sense that he first came to India and inspired his successors by his achievement. Humayun is important in that he managed to maintain the claim just long enough for others to be able to take over. The work of both would have been in vain if his successor had not possessed genius on his own account.' And that successor was Akbar who built an empire through conquest and diplomacy, established a working administration that filled the royal coffers with riches and created royal traditions that gave the Mughals nearly a divine status. The metropolis at Fatehpur Sikri was designed as the gorgeous stage for this imperial drama.

Abul Fazl quotes him as saying, 'a monarch should be ever intent on conquests; otherwise his neighbours rise in arms against him.' Akbar was first

▼ *Astrologer's Seat. This decorative kiosk stands before the Treasury, also called Ankh Michauli.*

and foremost an imperialist and his single minded policy was to extend the empire. He spent most of his life on military campaigns and like his grandfather Babur, he was a legendary warrior and inventive military strategist who never lost a battle. He was magnanimous once his power was acknowledged but he was merciless with those who defied him. Within a decade the borders of his kingdom stretched from Kabul in the northwest to Bengal in the east, Kashmir in the north and south to central India. Soon the southern kingdoms had acknowledged his suzerainty and the troublesome Rajput clans had been subdued either by alliances or by conquest.

To go back to the words of Percival Spear, 'Akbar's stroke was to raise himself from the position of a leader of a minority Indo-foreign group (the Muslims) to the accepted ruler of all Hindustan.' With Akbar we have the first Muslim king who won the allegiance of the Hindus and who's right to rule was not questioned by the people. There was peace in his kingdom, trade was booming and the treasury overflowed with gold and jewels. Within the first ten years of his reign he had become a supreme monarch and now the obsessive empire builder began to transform himself into a king.

◀ *Badshahi Darwaza. This gateway was used by Akbar to enter the Jami Masjid complex.*

A Saint on a Hill

In 1568 Akbar was twenty-six and a very worried man because he had no heir to inherit the empire that he was building. In spite of a harem full of queens and concubines none of his male children had survived. He was a devotee of the Sufi saint Khwaja Sheikh Muinuddin Chishti and often visited his shrine at Ajmer. In the spring of that year he went to Ajmer for prayers of thanksgiving after his victory over Chittor, when on his way back to Agra he heard of a living Sufi preacher, a recluse who lived in a shack on top of a hill at Sikri. Sheikh Salim was a member of the same Chishtiya order as Sheikh Muinuddin and Akbar promptly trudged up to pay his respects and seek his guidance.

▼ *Dargah of Sheikh Muinuddin Chishti at Ajmer. Akbar built a mosque, the Akbari Masjid, near the shrine.*

It was a meeting that filled Akbar's heart with hope, as Salim Chishti assured him that he would have not one but three living sons and within a few months he learnt that the princess of Amber was going to have a child. Popular tradition calls her Jodh Bai but no contemporary historian, not even Abul Fazl gives her a name. In the royal chronicles she is always referred to as the princess of Amber and then later, as the mother of the heir apparent, by her formal title of Mariam-us-Zamani. Akbar moved her into a palace that he built near the seminary of the saint at Sikri and on 30 August 1569 a son was born who was named Salim after the Sufi pir. When he became a king, Salim took the title of Jahangir and he writes in his memoirs that his father always called him Sheikhu Baba in the memory of the sheikh. Then the miracle continued and a second son Murad was born in 1570 and a third Daniyal in 1572. The Sufi's prediction had come true and for the grateful king, Salim Chishti became his personal saint, his symbol of good fortune and a spiritual guide.

The thanksgiving of a monarch can be a magnificent thing and Akbar was convinced that it was the saint's blessings that had saved his dynasty. So what did Akbar do to show his gratitude? In a gesture typical of a magnificent Mughal he built a city. Of course just gratitude was not enough and there was also an imperial imperative. By then his empire was at its zenith, the fortresses at Agra and Lahore were not grand enough and anyway, he liked building. So the time was right for founding a new city and where else but at an auspicious place like Sikri.

Akbar the Builder

From 1556 to 1571 Akbar's capital was at Agra and here he had built a new fortress by the River Yamuna and stamped the city with his imperial character. The Agra Fort was built at the site of an old Lodi citadel, where the existing brick structure was torn down and replaced with sandstone. As Abul Fazl wrote about this new fortress, that was started in 1565, 'Accordingly, he at this time gave directions for the building in Agra—which by its position in the centre of Hindustan—of a grand fortress such as might be worthy thereof, and correspond to the dignity of the dominions ... completed with all its battlements, breastwork and its loopholes, in the space of eight years under the faithful superintendence of Qasim Khan, Mir Barr-u-Bahr.' The fort became the heart of a flourishing city and for a long time after that, Agra was known as Akbarabad.

The red sandstone Agra Fort stands at a curve of the river and 4,000 labourers worked at the site. It was a fortress planned to face enemy attacks, with the river acting as a moat and with walls on the other three sides that rose up to 22 metres in height. On the city side a deep moat was laid between two layers of protective walls with drawbridges. It was designed in a crescent shape and the walls had battlements, embrasures and slits for the musketeers. Few looking at the forbidding walls and turrets could imagine the exquisite palaces and pavilions, marble fountains and gardens that stood inside. The Agra Fort established the model for all later Mughal forts, Akbar himself would build two more at Lahore and Allahabad and the last Mughal fort would be built by his grandson Shah Jahan at Delhi.

Unlike Fatehpur Sikri which remains a complete creation of Akbar, few palaces inside the Agra Fort are in the original Akbari style as Shah Jahan remodelled and rebuilt extensively here, covering many palaces in marble. One of the few that still show the architecture of his time is the Jahangiri Mahal that he is said to have built for his son. This is the earliest example of the delicate blend of Indian and Islamic architectural traditions that reached its epitome at Fatehpur Sikri. As the Jesuit Father Monserrate marvelled in 1580, 'The stones of these buildings are so cunningly fitted that the joints are scarcely visible, although no lime was used to fix them together. The beautiful colour of the stone, which is all red, also produces the same effect of uniform solidity.'

Akbar never really abandoned the Agra Fort. Even after Akbar had shifted to Fatehpur Sikri the well guarded fort remained the treasury of the kingdom and it was also the main citadel. Fatehpur Sikri was not planned to face a siege and Akbar would have

▼ *Agra Fort. Akbar demolished the Lodi Fort made of brick to build the grand fort in stone.*

had to retreat to the Agra Fort if he was attacked. The historian Badauni noted, 'After it was completed it became the depository and store house of all the gold of Hindustan.' It was from here that Akbar rode out to win an empire and when he rode away from Fatehpur Sikri in 1585, never to return, he continued to reside here. Later Jahangir ruled from here and Shah Jahan, dethroned by his son, spent his last days within its walls.

Most people forget about another monument that Akbar built because it was not erected in Agra. This was the mausoleum of his father Humayun in Delhi. Humayun had ruled and died at his fort Dinpanah by the banks of the River Yamuna in Delhi and it was near it that his garden tomb was built by the orders of Akbar. The Mughals loved gardens, fountains and the soothing charm of flowing water and these were always part of their buildings. Akbar wanted a tomb set in the middle of a landscaped garden in the Persian style and placed it near the shrine of another Sufi saint, Hazrat Nizamuddin Auliya.

Humayun's tomb was set in the middle of a charbagh garden and built in red sandstone with highlights in grey quartzite and marble. The massive

▼ *Humayun's Tomb. It was built under the supervision of one of Humayun's queens, Haji Begum.*

dome was covered in marble and there was the use of coloured tiles and white, black and yellow marble. It also had the first complete dome in the Persian style in India and the whole monument was framed by the arch of the gateway. Two things make the Humayun's Tomb special—one is its proximity to the dargah of a Sufi saint that gave it the same spiritual resonance as Fatehpur Sikri. Second and more importantly, it created the template for Mughal mausoleums, the 'tomb in a garden' and all of them would follow this design; the most famous being Shah Jahan's Taj Mahal.

Akbar laid the foundation of not just the administrative structure and religious policy but even court etiquette and culture. With the Agra Fort and Humayun's Tomb he began the process of evolving a Mughal style of architecture that would reach its heights with Shah Jahan. At Fatehpur Sikri this Akbari style of architecture and sculpture would blend with the arts, music and literature and make it a unique and courtly medieval city.

BUILDING FATEHPUR SIKRI

In 1571, when Akbar was in his fortieth year, after his yearly pilgrimage to Ajmer he halted at Sikri and in the words of Abul Fazl, 'Now that his standard had arrived at that place, his former design

▲ *The walls of Fatehpur Sikri were built with rubble with a covering of stone.*

was pressed forward and an order was issued that the superintendents of affairs should erect lofty buildings for the special use of the Shahinshah.'

The royal architects, masons, and stone carvers who had been labouring at Agra now moved into Sikri. The raw material for the palaces was easy to find, it was the red sandstone of the ridge at Sikri and from nearby Tantpur and Rupbas and it had already been used at the Agra Fort. With typical Akbari panache, the top of the hill was sliced off to create a flat area on which the complex of palaces came up with surprising speed. The city of palaces, pavilions, a mosque, a shrine, open courtyards, surrounding walls, was built with amazing rapidity and the royal family had moved in even before all the buildings had been completed.

Here is Abul Fazl describing the city in its heyday in his inimitable florid style, 'Fatehpur was a village ... situated twelve kos distant from Agra. After the accession of His Majesty, it rose to be a city of the first importance. A masonry fort was erected and two elephants carved in stone at its gate inspired astonishment. Several noble buildings also rose to completion and although the royal palace and the residences of many of the nobility

◀ *Diwan-i-Khas. The exterior view gives the impression of two stories when there is only one large, high ceilinged hall present.*

are upon the summit of the hill, the plains likewise are studded with numerous mansions and gardens. By the command of His Majesty a mosque, a college and a religious house were also built upon the hill, the like of which few travellers can name. In the neighbourhood is a tank, twelve kos is circumference, and on its embankment His Majesty constructed a spacious courtyard, a minar, and a place for the game of chaugan; elephant fights were also exhibited. In the vicinity is a quarry of red stone whence columns and slabs of any dimension can be excavated ... under His Majesty's patronage carpets and fine stuff are woven and numerous handicraftsmen have full occupation.' Abul Fazl gives a contemporary view and writes, 'There was a great city and there were charming palaces. Benevolent institutions such as khanquas (seminaries), schools and baths, were also constructed, and a large stone bazaar was built. Beautiful gardens were made in the vicinity. A place of great concourse was brought together such as might move the envy of the world.' The three princes Salim, Murad and Daniyal grew up here and Salim in his autobiography remembers these years as a happy time. What made Akbar's act unique was the impulse behind the decision. Any other king, when they raised gateways and palaces did it with the intention of

▶ *This colonnade creates a curtain of privacy between the public area and the harem.*

putting the stamp of their power and presence on the landscape. Akbar had done the same at the Agra Fort but at Fatehpur Sikri his guiding spirit was his gratitude to a penniless saint. As Jahangir remembers in his memoirs, 'My revered father, considering the village of Sikri, which was the place of my birth, lucky for him, made it his capital.'

There was gratitude, but Akbar was too astute and pragmatic a king to do anything for purely emotional reasons. The Mughal Empire deserved a more impressive capital than Agra Fort, it needed a whole city planned to celebrate his success. He was also an inveterate builder and felt that the empire was strong enough not to have the royal establishment barred behind the high walls of a citadel. It needed a courtly city where royal grandeur could be exhibited through the music of Tansen and the paintings of Daswant, the poetry of Faizi and the humour of Birbal, with elephant fights and games of chaugan. The Mughals, right from the time of Babur, had been fascinated by Timur's capital city, Samarkand and Akbar was going to create a similar architectural legend in India. His ambitious building plans reflected the immense wealth of the empire because even while Fatehpur Sikri was being built, work was still going on at the fortresses at Agra and Lahore. Akbar just never stopped building.

Around the main core of the royal palaces and mosque grew the other buildings—soldiers' barracks, stables for horses and elephants, administrative

▶ *A view of the courtyard and the pachisi board, the treasury on the left, Diwan-i-Khas in the centre.*

offices, quarters for servants, kitchens, an aqueduct for bringing water from the lake, wells, pools, the workshops of craftsmen and the royal mint. The usual practice in medieval times was that the king built the fortress and then the nobility built their mansions around it and soon markets and the homes of the poor sprang up in the outskirts. Here too the omrahs shifted their residence from Agra and built their havelis on the slope of the hill while the markets, factories, caravanserais and the plebeian homes of the common people came up at the bottom of the hill. As Abul Fazl writes, 'All grades of officers and the public generally made dwellings for themselves, and a high wall of stone and lime was placed around the place.'

Akbar's wish to be a true Indian king was also reflected in his architecture that evolved into a new indigenous style. All his craftsmen were Indian and mostly Hindu, many were stone carvers from Gujarat and they brought with them typically Hindu motifs like the lotus blossoms, leaves and vines, filigree screens and carved pillars. These were sensitively blended with Islamic domes and geometric and calligraphic patterns to create the elegant, airy buildings that visitors admire today. The style was of a refined simplicity that was so typical of Akbar who never chose ostentation over grandeur. As Louise Nicholson says, 'Taking Persian principles, he built and decorated in a very Indian way, inspired by such buildings as Gwalior Fort and served by Indian craftsmen.' It all held a sort of Akbari legerdemain, as if by a wave of his royal wand Akbar made a complete city appear on the landscape. Then to celebrate his

▲ *Panch Mahal. Every pillar here was carved in a different design.*

conquest of Gujarat he built the soaring gateway of the Buland Darwaza that dominates the mosque. Then he renamed his new city first as Fatehabad and then as Fatehpur—City of Victory.

In the evocative words of historian Abraham Eraly, 'Built on a rocky ridge of the Aravalli range, Sikri is quintessentially Akbarian in ethos. It is robust and sinewy, without the self-conscious aestheticism of Jahangir or the cloying sweetness of Shah Jahan, Sikri throbs with power and vitality. Yet, there is also an unmistakable air of mystery about Sikri. Its layout is complex and confusing, the function of many of its structures unknown, the reason for their curious designs unfathomable. Several different architectural and decorative styles interwove in Sikri, and that too was very much in the character of Akbar. The unity of Sikri is more of character and spirit than of architectural style.'

Akbar liked to get involved, so he set up camp at Sikri, and supervised the building work and wandered about the site. The work went on at an amazing pace and one of the reasons could have been the constant presence of the king. There are miniature paintings showing him with masons, stone carvers and labourers and Father Monserrate writes, 'Zelaldinus (Jalaluddin) is so devoted to building that he sometimes quarries himself along with other

▲ *A view of the Panch Mahal from Akbar's personal palace, the Khwabgah.*

workmen. Nor does he shrink from watching, and even practising, for the sake of amusement, the craft of an ordinary artisan.' Most of the important palaces were ready for occupation within two years and in the words of Jahangir, 'That hill full of wild beasts became a city containing all kinds of gardens and buildings, lofty edifices and pleasant palaces attractive to the heart.'

Wandering through the ghostly colonnades and the shadowy rooms of the palaces it is easy to imagine what it must have been like when it was alive with people. Noblemen—the rajas and amirs, in their gorgeous clothes walking busily through the courtyards, soldiers standing guard at the gateways, busy officials sitting cross legged on cushions, bent over their low desks scribbling in big ledgers. Then to shouted orders, the roll of drums and men bowing, Akbar would arrive to give an audience at the Diwan-i-Aam. He would come and sit on the square seat, resplendent in silks and jewels, lean back against the bolsters and listen to the petitions of his subjects as they gathered in the courtyard before him.

Leaving the City

Akbar, ambitious conqueror and a restless traveller was not a man to stay at one place for long. He and his court stayed at Fatehpur Sikri for fourteen years and then in 1585 he left for the Punjab on a long military expedition against a rebellious half brother. Then he visited Kashmir a number of times and only returned to Agra for a long stay in 1598. Once he was back in the capital he chose to stay at the old citadel of the Agra Fort and not Fatehpur Sikri and except for a few short months, he never went back there again. The reason for this abandonment of a city that he had built with such personal involvement has intrigued many and none of the contemporary chronicles give an explanation.

The city was abandoned by its citizens soon after Akbar left in 1585 and except for the main palaces most of the buildings rapidly degenerated into ruins. The English traveller Ralph Fitch who arrived in India in 1608, just three years after the death of Akbar writes, 'It is all ruinate, lying like a waste desert, and very dangerous to pass through in the night, the buildings lying waste without inhabitants; much of the ground being now converted gardens, and much sowed with nill and other grain, that a man standing there would little think he were in the middest of a citie.'

As the years went by, the courtyards lay silent in the sun, the palaces waited for the monarch's footsteps and the gateways no longer echoed to the clash of arms. The streets did not light up with royal processions and the mosque came alive only during prayers. Only the

pilgrims never forgot Sheikh Salim Chishti, they kept arriving, bearing their hopes and prayers. But then as dusk fell and the people left, the city was silent once again. Akbar turned away and Fatehpur Sikri became the most beautiful ghost town in the world.

Historians have speculated energetically about the mystery of Fatehpur Sikri. One theory is that the water supply failed as the lake either dried up during a drought or was not adequate enough. This is hard to believe as Akbar's architects

▲ *Diwan-i-Aam. It was set within a courtyard surrounded by a colonnade.*

and town planners would not have ignored such a basic requirement for a city. Also travellers who visited the area after Akbar mention the presence of a large lake. The city was amply provided with an aqueduct, water tanks and wells and there was an artificial lake at the bottom of the hill. Some of the tanks and wells survive till today. You can walk on the surface of the original natural lake as it has dried up and now is a stretch of fields. Also, all through the years when the court functioned from here, Agra continued to be part of the imperial axis and it was in fact a twin city.

One reason for Akbar choosing to stay at Agra Fort till his death may have been the fact that Fatehpur Sikri was not a citadel. It was planned as an open, courtly city and therefore it would have been hard to defend. The latter half of Akbar's reign was a time of turmoil when he first faced the rebellion of his half brother Mirza Muhammad Hakim who was the governor of Kabul. Hakim had the covert support of the Uzbeg noblemen in the royal court and the king had to march north to quell the rebellion. The Afghan nobility in Bengal often gave him problems and there were the conquests of Umarkot, Baluchistan and Kandahar and an intermittent campaign to the Deccan that went on for twelve years. Finally his elder son Salim was in a state of sporadic revolt for many years. As John Richards says, 'The lovely palaces of Fatehpur Sikri were not suited to the grim realities that confronted an aging emperor coping with an ambitious son.' So the simple reason could be that Akbar felt safer in the Agra Fort that held the royal garrison and the imperial treasury.

Also we think of empires having a single capital city but in Mughal times the capital was where the king set down his royal tent. As historian Abraham Eraly writes, 'Agra, Delhi and Fatehpur Sikri

were Mughal capitals only in a formal sense, for the imperial capital was in effect wherever the emperor was encamped for some length of time, as the entire governmental machinery moved with him, with all the essential records and treasures.' It reminds one of the colonial British government shifting yearly—bag, baggage and departmental files—from Delhi to Simla during the summer months.

Akbar built at Agra, Lahore and Allahabad but among all his creations it is Fatehpur Sikri that retains the strongest flavour of a bygone era. It stands away from the cities of modern India on an isolated hill and without the intrusion of people it has retained its unique character. It is like the stage of an imperial theatre faithfully recreating the splendour of the court of one of the greatest kings of India. In Fatehpur Sikri, Akbar has his finest epitaph.

▼ *The walls of Fatehpur Sikri are visible from far along the road from Agra.*

A Man called Akbar

Four centuries after he died Jalaluddin Akbar continues to fascinate people. He has not been forgotten till date by the world and is often listed among people who played a seminal role in world history. Behind the gorgeous portraits and legendary exploits what was this man called Akbar really like?

Akbar's character comes vividly to life while reading the chronicle of the period, not just the admiring, worshipful words of his royal historian Abul Fazl but also the more cynical writings of Badauni and the memoirs of travellers like Father Monserrate and Ralph Fitch. Akbar's vividly faceted character and quicksilver mind is not easy to capture in a few words and like all great men he was an intriguing mix of the ordinary and the remarkable. This was a man who became king at thirteen and survived many challenges to the throne, including two assassination attempts, built an immense empire and ruled as the unquestioned monarch for nearly fifty years. These are achievements that needed some very special qualities of head and heart.

He was a true leader of men who inspired absolute loyalty among his nobility, bureaucracy and generals. As a warrior he fought with reckless courage, often putting his life in danger and as a general he always led his men into battle and was a shrewd and ruthless military strategist who never lost a war. He was

▶ *Diwan-i-Khas. The top of the pillar with the delicate serpentine brackets.*

a tough energetic man who enjoyed taking physical risks—playing polo, riding wild elephants, taming horses and facing tigers during a hunt. He was also a pragmatic and inventive administrator who set up economic and revenue systems that lasted for centuries. A large part of his life was of course spent going to war, which meant arduous expeditions in all kinds of weather through the roughest of terrains and then the stress and danger of battle. Akbar revelled in it and would lead an expedition to the far off Deccan even when he was in his sixties.

He was an obsessively organised and extremely hard working king and his daily work schedule would have exhausted most men. He slept only for three or four hours at night and ate just one meal a day. The rest of the time was spent in the work of the empire. As his son Jahangir recollects, 'His nights were passed in wakefulness; and in the day too he slept little, so that the total period of sleep in night-and-day did not exceed four-and-a-half hours. He treated wakefulness at night as something gained out of the given lifetime.' As a matter of fact, in spite of their image as luxury-loving oriental potentates, all the early Mughal kings, from Babur to Aurangzeb, worked very hard and among the most meticulous and conscientious were Akbar and later his great grandson Aurangzeb.

▼ *A rare human figure carved on a wall in the Haramsara.*

▲ *Diwan-i-Aam. At this public audience chamber the common people could approach the king.*

Abul Fazl's detailed records in the *Akbarnama* give us a pretty good idea of a day in the life of Badshah Akbar at Fatehpur Sikri. It began at dawn with him sitting at a palace window to show himself to his subjects who gathered below. This ceremony called Jharokha-i-Darshan was invented by him and served the purpose of telling the people that he was alive and well and also gave them an opportunity to approach him directly.

Then he moved down from his bed chamber to the ground floor offices where he got his first reports from his bureaucrats. Next there was the more formal public audience at the Diwan-i-Aam to listen to petitions and pass judgements. Then to the roll of drums he moved to the Diwan-i-Khas for private audiences, where he received ambassadors, provincial governors and vassal kings, listened to reports and took decisions on state matters. On some days he inspected the royal horses and elephants, on others he visited the karkhanas, the royal workshops for painters, stone and metal carvers, carpet and textile weavers.

He was always easily accessible to people and Father Monserrate who observed him closely at Fatehpur Sikri writes, 'He creates an opportunity almost everyday for any of the common people or the nobles to see him and converse with him.' After lunch, which was his only proper meal of the day and he usually took to the harem, he relaxed for a while and then went back to work, with his officials reading out reports. In the evening there may be some entertainment like music or dancing, animal fights and games. Akbar employed spies, stationed all across the kingdom and he personally heard their reports at night and then just before going to bed he always listened to readings from books.

He was inherently a humane and just man who made sure he did not lose touch with his subjects and as a young king was known to have wandered about anonymously in Agra meeting common people and even getting into trouble a couple of times. At the same time he was an absolute monarch who expected unquestioned obedience from everyone and if defied he could be fearful in his anger. He took great pride in being just and there are only a few examples, like his sacking of Chittor, when he behaved with any unnatural cruelty. For a medieval monarch he was remarkably free from religious prejudices and for the first time in India, a Muslim king welcomed Hindus into the inner circle of friends and advisers.

In the Ibadat Khana, where he gathered the scholars of many religions, he was probably the only person who was genuinely free of religious prejudice and simply interested in all faiths. He was most influenced by liberal thinkers like the Sufis Sheikh Mubarak and Sheikh Tajuddin and by the Zoroastrian scholar Mahyarji Rana. He was trying to delink religion from the state and that was a remarkable effort in medieval times. Like most of his actions his religious policy too was based more on pragmatic reality than on any passionately held beliefs. He wanted peace in the kingdom, the support of all his people and he wanted the king to be the supreme authority to his subjects, not the mullahs.

For Akbar the empire and the dynasty always came first and historian Percival Spear analysing the qualities that made him such a successful king writes, 'Leadership, however inspired is not enough; it has to be creative leadership if it is to charm a mixed people to cooperate in goodwill rather than acquiesce through fear. Akbar's stroke was to raise himself from the position of a leader of a minority Indo-foreign group (the Muslims) to the accepted ruler of all Hindustan.'

In spite of being a despot there was also a genuine humanity in him and he was always willing to reward ability and talent. He appointed a man belonging to the untouchable Chandal caste as the head of his palace guards and gave him the title of Khidmat Rai and one of his miniature painters, Daswant was the son of a poor *palki* bearer. He sincerely believed that the welfare of his subjects was his responsibility and it was

◀ *Diwan-i-Khas. Historians still puzzle over the real purpose of this palace with a very idiosyncratic design.*

this generous spirit that transformed him from being the leader of a minority ruling elite to a popular king of Hindustan. He wrote to his son Murad about the responsibilities of a ruler, 'Let not differences of religion interfere with policy, and be not violent in inflicting retribution. Adorn the confidential council with men who know their work. If apologies be made, accept them.' For every Indian he was their own monarch and even as late as 1857, when North India rose against the British it was in the name of the Mughals.

He was a voraciously curious man and there was a hunger for knowledge about everything from sports and horses to how a palace is built or a carpet is woven. Father Monserrate writes, 'The king is considered by some to be mad because he is very dextrous in all jobs, because I have seen him making ribbons like a lace maker, and filing, sawing, and working very hard. He watches and even practises, for the sake of amusement, the craft of an ordinary artisan.' Though functionally illiterate, he loved books, built up an immense library and got books in Sanskrit translated including the *Mahabharata*.

Our image of the pomp and pageantry of the Mughal court with its rigid etiquette and courtly style was something Akbar created. He would sit resplendent in silks and jewels, the nobles gathered before him and there were the dramatic rituals of elaborate bowing and presenting of gifts, the loud announcements, the beating of drums and blowing of trumpets. It was Akbar who invented this super human, semi-divine monarch

▶ *Agra Fort. For the first time the walls and gateways were built exclusively in stone.*

◀ *Akbari Masjid. The architecture of the Akbari period relied on clean, elegant lines and a subtle use of carvings.*

whose portraits had a halo around the head. He was an unapologetic imperialist and what came to be known as the 'Mughalia' culture was often a product of Akbar's fertile mind.

Finally Akbar as he was remembered by his son Jahangir, 'Although he was illiterate, so much became clear to him through constant intercourse with the learned and wise, that from his conversations with them, no one could take him to be illiterate. And he was so well acquainted with the niceties of verse and prose compositions that such deficiency could not be imagined.'

Then he describes his father, 'In his august personal appearance he was of middle height, but inclining to be tall; he was of wheatish complexion, his eyes and eyebrows were black and his features were more refined than (merely) handsome, he was slender waisted with a broad chest, and his hands and arms were long. On the left side of his nose he had a fleshy mole, very agreeable in appearance, of the size of half a common pea. Those skilled in the science of physiognomy considered this mole a sign of great prosperity and exceeding good fortune. His august voice was very resonant and in speech and discourse was very well modulated. In his actions and movements he was not like the people of this world, and the light of God emanated from him.'

Timeline of Akbar's Reign

The life of Akbar reads like an adventure tale with a hero who never lost a battle in his life. When Akbar came to the throne at the age of thirteen his kingdom only included the cities of Delhi and Agra. When he died its boundaries stretched from the Deccan in the south to Kabul in the north. He also united a people of diverse religions and cultures and created a truly Indian empire. Babur laid the foundation of the kingdom but it is Akbar's energetic life that created the magnificent Mughal Empire that became a legend across the world.

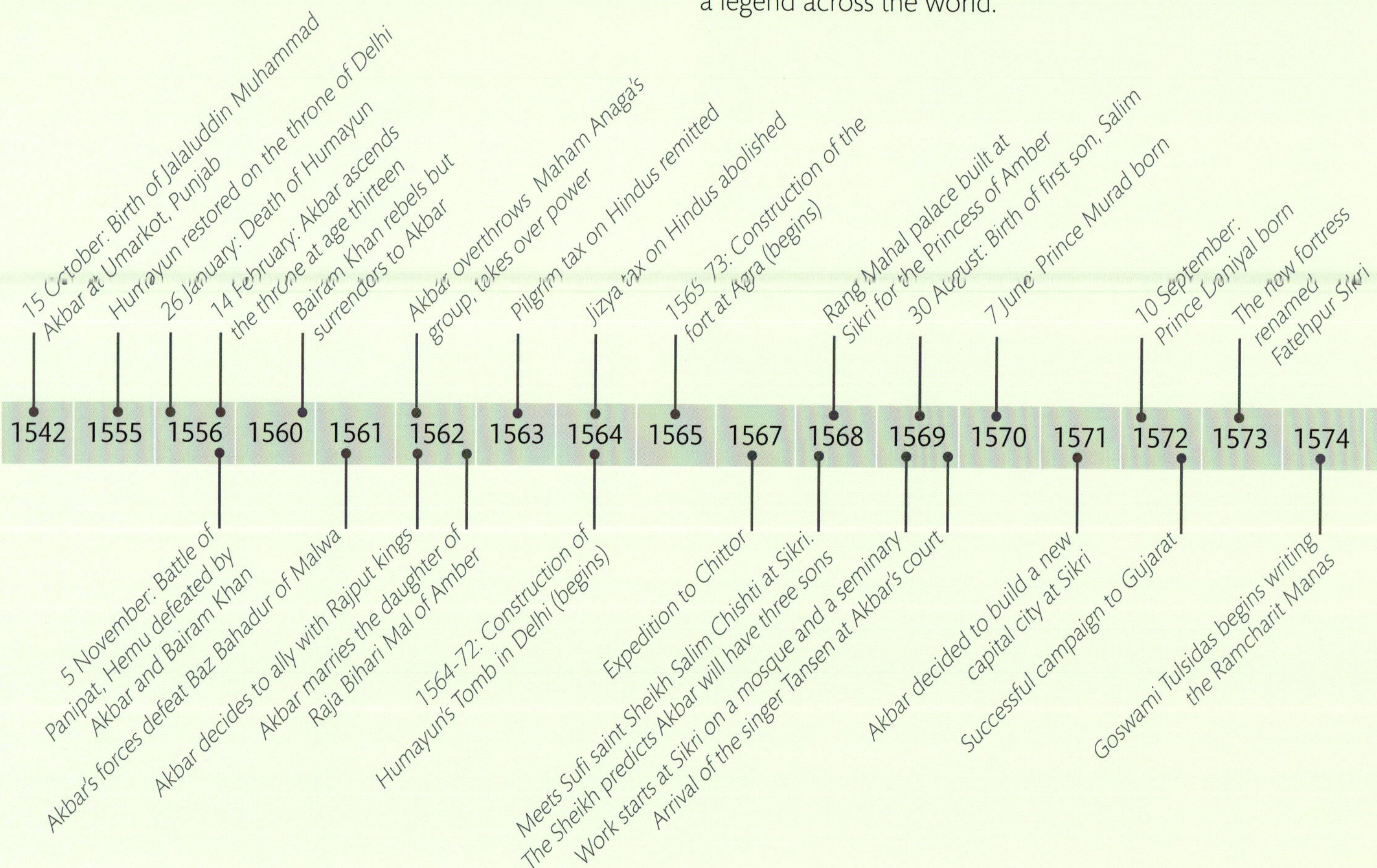

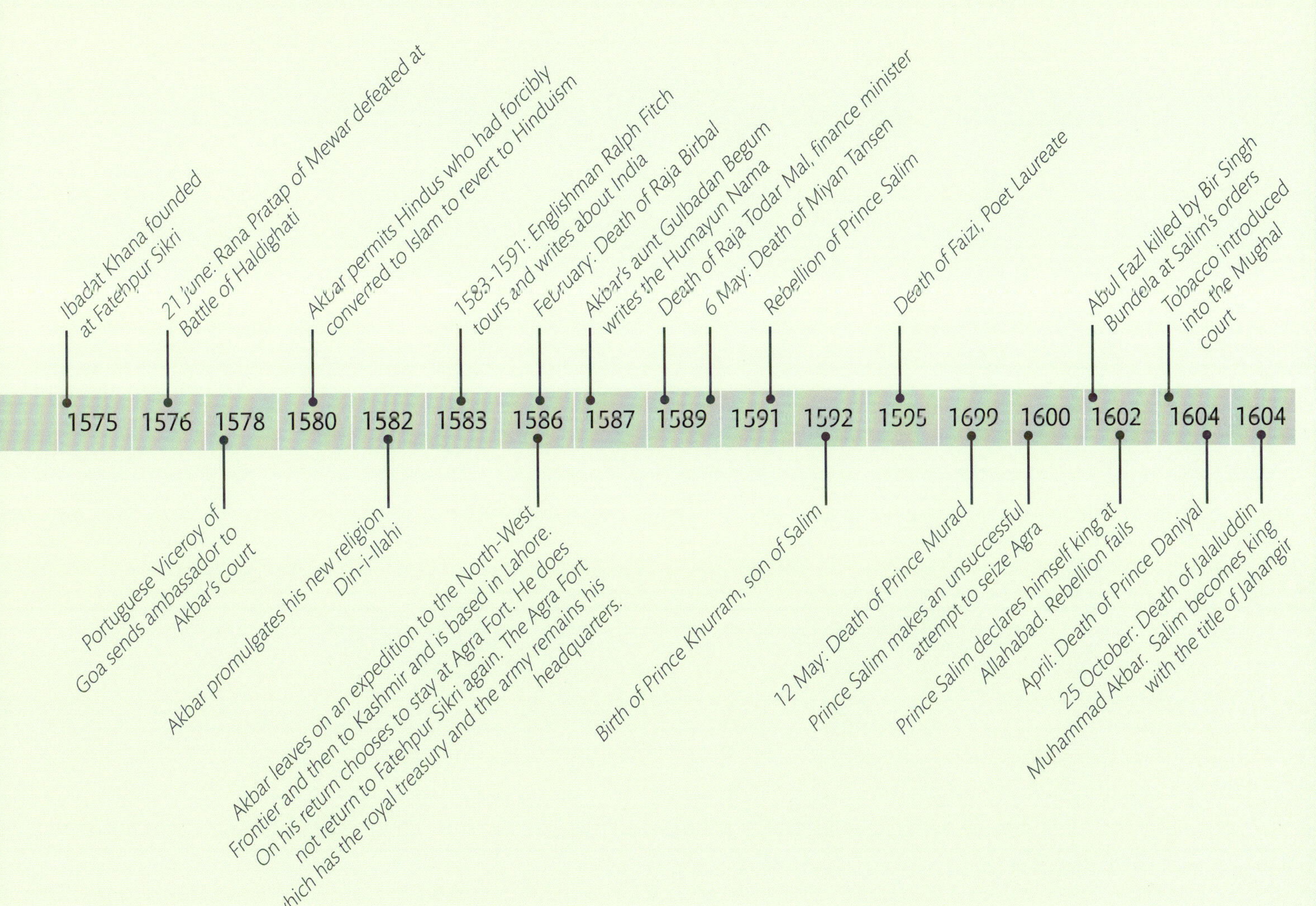
1575
Ibadat Khana founded at Fatehpur Sikri
1576
21 June: Rana Pratap of Mewar defeated at Battle of Haldighati
1578
Portuguese Viceroy of Goa sends ambassador to Akbar's court
1580
Akbar permits Hindus who had forcibly converted to Islam to revert to Hinduism
1582
Akbar promulgates his new religion Din-i-Ilahi
1583
1583-1591: Englishman Ralph Fitch tours and writes about India
1586
February: Death of Raja Birbal
Akbar leaves on an expedition to the North-West Frontier and then to Kashmir and is based in Lahore. On his return chooses to stay at Agra Fort. He does not return to Fatehpur Sikri again. The Agra Fort which has the royal treasury and the army remains his headquarters.
1587
Akbar's aunt Gulbadan Begum writes the Humayun Nama
1589
Death of Raja Todar Mal, finance minister
6 May: Death of Miyan Tansen
1591
Rebellion of Prince Salim
1592
Birth of Prince Khuram, son of Salim
1595
Death of Faizi, Poet Laureate
1699
12 May: Death of Prince Murad
1600
Prince Salim makes an unsuccessful attempt to seize Agra
1602
Abul Fazl killed by Bir Singh Bundela at Salim's orders
Prince Salim declares himself king at Allahabad. Rebellion fails
1604
Tobacco introduced into the Mughal court
April: Death of Prince Daniyal
1604
25 October: Death of Jalaluddin Muhammad Akbar. Salim becomes king with the title of Jahangir

THE IMPERIAL CENTRE

The imperial centre

'Mighty fortresses have been raised, which protect the timid, frighten the rebellious, and please the obedient. Delightful villas, and imposing towers have also been built. They afford excellent protection against cold and rain, provide for the comfort of the princesses of the harem, and are conducive to that dignity which is so necessary for worldly power.'

-Abul Fazl, *Akbarnama*

Babur was in India for barely four years and could only plan a few garden pavilions. Humayun's tumultuous reign gave him no respite for the peaceful pastime of building and all he managed to build was the walls of the fortress that he had optimistically named Din Panah. So it was left to the third king of the dynasty who had the interest, the wealth and the time to leave his imperial stamp on the landscape by building fortresses, mausoleums, palaces, mosques and finally an entire city. It is thus, Jalaluddin Akbar who laid the true foundation of not just the Mughal Empire, but also the tradition of Mughal architecture that still dazzles the world. The Taj Mahal may be the visual symbol of the dynasty but to appreciate it better you have to see where it all started—at Fatehpur Sikri.

In the sixteenth century, Islamic architecture was nothing new in India. Sultans had been ruling from their seat in Delhi for 300 years and there were Muslim kingdoms in the Deccan. What we call Mughal architecture is in fact a continuation of the design traditions that the Delhi sultans and provincial powers like Jaunpur, Golconda and Bijapur had begun. What the Mughals added was a flamboyant grandeur

◀ *Sunahra Makan. An arched niche carved on a wall.*

through lavish spending, a sophisticated aesthetic sense and a highly original synthesis with the ancient Hindu traditions that began through the inspiration of Akbar. It would reach its apogee with Shah Jahan's building the Taj Mahal—a tomb that was envisaged all in marble and then decorated like a piece of jewellery with semi-precious gems.

When on a trip to Agra to experience the dazzling allure of the Taj Mahal, a visit to Fatehpur Sikri gives the visitor a glimpse into the beginnings of what we call Mughal architecture. It is like a template for all that was to follow and at the core of its magic was the original mind, abundant creative energy and spirit of catholicity of Akbar.

In a Mughal Style

When we say Akbar built a city it does give a slightly wrong impression. A planned city with a precisely laid out grid of roads and division of localities, was not created at Fatehpur Sikri. The usual medieval way of starting a new urban centre was for the king to build the walled citadel, palaces, mosques, tombs and may be lay out the main bazaar and a few gardens. After that the city grew, sort of on its own, around this core. It is only when Shah Jahan built his new capital city in Delhi that he laid out the main areas of the metropolis in a more systematic manner. At Fatehpur Sikri what Akbar built was a walled fortress pierced by gateways, a royal complex of palaces and offices, a mosque and the tomb of Salim Chishti. As architectural historian

▲ *The Taj Mahal. Built by Akbar's grandson Shah Jahan and considered the finest Mughal creation.*

J. C. Harle says, 'The Fatehpur Sikri visited by tourists today is a palace with a very large mosque rather than a city.' The rest of the city grew in an

unplanned manner around the palaces. The omrah from the court built their havelis along the slope of the hill and the ragged shops and homes of the poor sprang up along a labyrinth of narrow, twisting lanes below it. And we had a typical medieval Indian city.

The Mughals built the giant gateways, imposing fortresses and indulgent palaces not just for their own use, there was a clearly defined political aspect to the constructions. Through these buildings they were asserting their might over the kingdom. As historian G. H .R. Tillotson comments,

'They served as emblems of power and wealth, designed to dazzle and cow the native rajas who attended the overlord's court.' During Akbar's reign when the fortresses rose at Agra, Lahore, Allahabad and Fatehpur Sikri, the underlying message was that the Mughals may have come as conquerors but they were here to stay. Akbar was not the sort to be apologetic about his imperial designs and he was going to leave his royal imprint on the land with a defiant arrogance.

Standing below the imposing bulk of the Buland Darwaza you can hear the message that Akbar was broadcasting through every carved archway. He was the unquestioned monarch of all he surveyed and even the slightest of opposition would be put down with a ruthless hand. Mughal architecture was many things—an elegant synthesis of the various Indian styles blended with Persian traditions, inspired by the inclusive and liberal temperament of the kings and the imaginative flair of the craftsmen. However, like the British creation of New Delhi, first and foremost the architecture is imperial.

Akbar was the trendsetter of the dynasty in many other ways. He created the elaborate court etiquette that his descendents refined upon. He enjoyed dressing up, starting fashions in clothes and was said to have one thousand sets of clothes stitched every year. In the same way he began the style that we now call Mughal architecture. He lavished a huge amount of money on his building programme. He was

▶ *Buland Darwaza. Viewed from the courtyard of the Jami Masjid.*

◀ *Buland Darwaza. It was embellished by quotations carved in delicate calligraphy and geometric patterns.*

▼ *Buland Darwaza. The marble inlay patterns add a touch of lightness to the red sandstone.*

always open to ideas and the style that evolved during his reign was not strictly an Islamic one. As you wander around the shadowy courtyard of Jodh Bai's palace or admire the intricate carvings on the pillars of the Turkish Sultana's pavilion you can spot both Islamic arches and Hindu brackets and motifs. Then the designs of the Diwan-i-Aam or the Panch Mahal have an idiosyncratic oddity that is never repeated in later architecture. It is very easy to sense that these were inspired by the aesthetic impulses of one man—Akbar himself.

▼ *Buland Darwaza. A close up of calligraphy, floral and geometric motifs.*

A Beautiful Synthesis

No one knows the name of the real creators of these palaces and pavilions—the stone carver, masons, architects or the artists who drew the patterns for the carvings. As in all royal architecture, the credit is given solely to the patron and king and the artists remain anonymous and are soon forgotten. This neglect of the Indian artist can be traced back to the low social status of craftspeople in Hindu society. The sculptor, wood carver, painter, weaver or potter are relegated to the lower castes and their contributions are never acknowledged.

Another reason for their anonymity was that most creative work was a cooperative enterprise. For instance, a Mughal miniature painting could be the work of three or four artists—with one man sketching in the figures, another doing the faces and the third colouring it—the design and construction of a palace would be the work of a group. To go back to Tillotson, 'The design process involved a hierarchy of craftsmen, with various grades of skills but there was no essential distinction between the functions of designer and builder: unlike in contemporary Europe, the men who worked the stone were executing their own, not other men's ideas.' It led to a typical Indian spirit of variety and a rejection of uniformity, where each pillar in a palace would be subtly different from each other in the carvings.

◀ *Astrologer's Seat. The toran design of the brackets is the work of craftsmen from Gujarat.*

▲ *Turkish Sultana's Palace. Carved panel on the wall with delicately chiselled motifs inspired by nature.*

How Islamic is Mughal architecture? Babur arrived from Kabul still carrying his dream of the blue tiled mosques and mausoleums of Samarkand. Humayun spent some time in the court of Shah Tahmasp and travelled around the Persian kingdom. Did that mean the Mughals would transfer Central Asian and Persian traditions to India? In fact Akbar did not construct a single building that could be marked as completely alien to India because he clearly did not acknowledge any aesthetic connections outside the country. Akbar was by political instinct and personal preference, an Indian monarch. Also except for Aurangzeb all the Mughals ignored the strict Islamic strictures against figurative depictions. Their buildings are covered with motifs taken from nature—flowers, leaves, vines and fruit, clouds and birds. Akbar even put up two full sized figures of the Rajput warriors Jaimal and Patta at the gates of Agra Fort and both he and Jahangir encouraged their painter to illustrate manuscripts with scenes from life. And all the Mughal emperors enjoyed their portraits being painted often with the rather provocative celestial halo encircling their heads.

▲ *Panch Mahal. There are a variety of sculptural details on the pillars and the balcony screens.*

There are Indian, Islamic and foreign elements in Mughal architecture as the Mughal court was a magnet for the finest talents of the Islamic world and the craftsmen of India. The on-site craftsmen were mostly Indian, so even if a pavilion was planned by a Persian architect the actual work would be done by Indians who wove their own craft traditions into the design, and thus various streams of creativity came into play. The Hindu and Buddhist carvings had intricate figurative designs—flowers and vines, animals and birds in a sort of profuse anarchy. In contrast there was the Islamic tradition that disapproved of figurative patterns and concentrated on an ascetic geometric symmetry. At Fatehpur Sikri, under the benign eye of the king these two styles were blended together to create an elegant, majestic fusion. Or in the effusive language of Abul Fazl, 'His Majesty plans splendid edifices, and dresses the work of his mind and art in the garment of stone and clay.'

There was some synthesis during the time of the sultans but rather inadvertently as they also used Indian craftsmen. With Akbar the vital difference was that the synthesis was deliberate as he was an enthusiastic supporter of everything Indian. Humayun's Tomb in Delhi is probably the only Akbari building that is Persian in spirit because by the time of the work at Sikri he exhibited a clear preference for the Hindu trabeate style which uses beams, brackets and corbel and not arches. Producing what S. K. Saraswati calls a 'fresh and virile' style imbued with a 'spirit of catholicity'.

So just as he enjoyed wearing *dhotis*, putting a *tilak* on his forehead, listening to Tansen sing a raga and celebrate Deepavali, Akbar also allowed his craftsmen greater freedom to incorporate Hindu designs into the architecture. The typical pointed arch or the double dome and the formal charbagh gardens were imported from the Islamic world. So was the building of open pillared pavilions instead of the closed, dim palaces that Hindus built with rooms where the

▼ *The open pavilions all have decorative pillars with carved bases.*

▼ *A detail of the floral carving often used at the base of pillars in most Mughal buildings*

sunlight never penetrated. The plan of the palaces was Central Asian, reflecting the tents of the nomads which were then ornamented with Hindu motifs. The curving *bangaldar* roof, the intricately carved pillars teeming with motifs from nature, the rounded domed kiosks called *chhatris* in the corners of terraces, the *chhajas* that are the overhanging eaves are all Indian. What he produced was in Eraly's words, 'Robust and sinewy, without the self-conscious aestheticism of Jahangir or the cloying sweetness of Shah Jahan, Sikri throbs with power and vitality.' If you study them carefully you will spot how Jodh Bai's palace has clearly defined Gujarati features and the Turkish Sultana's pavilion reflects the wooden architecture of the Punjab. The painted walls of the Sunahra Makan and Khwabgah are reminiscent of Buddhist traditions. As historian Eraly says, 'Akbar drew strength and inspiration from the land and the people he ruled.' It

▼ *The pillars in the Haramsara show a variety of carved designs*

▼ *The design of pillars and beams are the traditional Hindu trabeate design.*

is the Indian spirit that is supreme in Fatehpur Sikri and what Akbar achieved was an architectural style that was not Persian, Central Asian, Islamic, Buddhist or Hindu. It was Mughal.

Planning a Citadel

The fortress walls encircle the top of the hill at Fatehpur Sikri and it is strewn with buildings—palaces, pavilions, rows of arcades and colonnades. The more important ones have names, often the imaginative creations of tourist guides in the nineteenth century and many others are nameless and their purpose can only be guessed at. What is clear is that the whole complex—of the king's public palaces, his residential pavilions, the harem and the offices were all laid out to a precise plan.

One can sense that in the way one's movement is controlled through carefully laid down pathways that lead to specific areas from the Badshahi Darwaza—first the public audience chamber the Diwan-i-Aam, then to the private one—the Diwan-i-Khas, then to Akbar's personal palace, the Khwabgah and then behind a screen the Haramsara. It is also created for the requirement and convenience of a single man—the monarch. One senses the plan but as there are no contemporary records or architectural drawings one can only make educated guesses about the purpose of many of the

▶ *Daulat Khana-i-Khas. No contemporary historian identified the buildings in the imperial centre.*

'His table is very sumptuous, generally consisting of more than forty courses served in great dishes. These are brought into the royal dining-hall covered and wrapped in linen cloths...They are carried by youths to the door of the dining-hall, other servants walking ahead and the master-of-the-household following. Here they are taken over by eunuchs, who hand them to the serving girls who wait on the royal table. He is accustomed to dine in private, except on the occasion of a public banquet.'

***Father Antonio Monserrate** on Akbar's table.*

▼ *Sunahra Makan. One of the rare figurive carvings at Fatehpur Sikri.*

▼ *Haramsara. After the Agra Fort the quality of the carvings became finer and more sophisticated at Fatehpur Sikri.*

▲ *Jami Masjid. Here the low dome of the mosque was hidden behind a row of chhtaris.*

buildings. The citadel can be divided into two main areas—the personal domain of the king with support structures like offices, soldier's quarters, stables, baths and kitchens. The other is the spiritual area with a large congregational mosque, the giant gateway and the tomb of the Sufi saint Sheikh Salim Chishti.

The two most trusted royal chroniclers Abul Fazl and Arif Qandhari state that the emperor ordered the work to start in 1571, when Prince Salim was two years old. It is as if Akbar, who had lost a number of infant children, waited to see if this son would survive.

The main core of the fortress was ready in a remarkably short time, Akbar had started staying there in a small palace right from the start and the royal family moved in within a couple of years. The work of building of course went on for fifteen years and even that is quite a short span of time for building a fortress. It went on simultaneously at many sites and that is only possible if an overall city plan had been prepared first.

Historian Glenn D. Lowry who has studied the layout of the fortress writes, 'Seen from the lake, Fatehpur Sikri's plan takes on coherence invisible from the western approach along the main road.' Gateways lead into important areas like the Diwan-i-Aam where the public gathered before the king. Paths circumvent the private palaces of the royal family and go towards the offices of the Daftar Khana that was placed behind Akbar's residence, the Khwabgah and at an easy walking distance. There are public baths near the caravanserais, shops that hug the main walls so that the people living in the citadel had an easy access to them and screened colonnades hide the harem.

Historian Irfan Habib has studied an aspect of the building of Fatehpur Sikri few have done before. How much did it cost to build this monumental symbol of Akbar's power and prestige? As he writes, 'The impressive scale of construction alone demanded a considerable investment of resources all made within a period of almost sixteen years.' He then digs out some fascinating numbers. Jahangir wrote in his memoirs, the Tuzuk-i-Jahangiri, that the Great Mosque and the Buland Darwaza cost half a million or five lakh rupees. According to the Dutch traveller Francisco Pelsaert, the palaces and the wall cost one and a half million or fifteen lakh rupees. Of course it was something Akbar could well afford as his share of the annual revenue, after claims of the nobility and other expenditure just in the year 1580 was fifteen million or one and a half crore rupees. As Habib writes with a touch of irony, 'We may be sure that, relatively speaking, the building-work at Sikri alone could hardly have put the emperor's resources to much strain.' He calculates that between 5000 to 8000 workers were employed at the site. These included master stone cutters,

masons and labourers who carried the earth and stone. Then there were the workmen employed by the omrahs who had been ordered to shift from Agra to Fatehpur Sikri and were constructing their brick and lime plaster havelis beyond the fortress walls. He estimates that at its busiest time over 20,000 people were at work building the city and the population

▼ *The Mughals introduced the Persian charbagh landscaped garden into India.*

of Fatehpur Sikri in the 1580s when it was at its zenith, was at about 220,000 people and we have to remember that it was more than the population of London at that time.

Abraham Eraly sums up Akbar's concept of architecture beautifully, he 'bypassed the derivative idiom and created a vigorously original architectural style of his own, by synthesising Persian and Indian traditions—Indian in its construction methods, intricacy of ornamentation and overall ambience, but Persian in its openness and expansiveness, it was the self-expression of a blessedly inspired and daring monarch, who, unrestrained by convention, could journey into the unknown with the confidence that time and fortune, wealth and power, abided with him.'

▼ *A small building by the entrance of Jodh Bai's Palace often called her kitchen but probably a guard house.*

Abul Fazl writes that once Akbar filled the Anup Talao with coins of 'copper, silver and gold' and distributed an amount equal to 1.67 million rupees.

THE DAULAT KHANA-I-KHAS

A King's Domain

Sheikh Salim Chishti died in 1572, a year after the building work began at Fatehpur Sikri. He was buried in a tomb in the courtyard of the congregational mosque, the Jami Masjid that was still being built. Akbar built the royal complex of palaces where he

▼ *Jami Masjid. The interiors of the mosque show a variety of decorative styles.*

'Often he comes out in ordinary dress and mixes with his confidants and makes no distinction between companions and strangers...Indeed, once I saw him flying a kite on the roof of his own palace; his head was bare and he was wearing a loin cloth (lungi). From this I was convinced that His Majesty was of an open bent of mind and extremely informal.'

Rafi-ud-din Shirazi*, the Persian traveller who came to India in 1559 on Akbar's convivial character.*

lived and worked right next to the spiritual heart of his new city. In this way he was always within the benign aura of his beloved Sufi saint and could also walk across easily to pray at the dargah whenever his spirit needed the succour of prayer. The palaces were placed around courtyards and their open, pillared halls often resembled the elaborate tents of the imperial camp. They were all built with the red sandstone brought from nearby Tantpur, Rupbas and also quarried from the Sikri ridge itself.

The palaces and the mosque stand on top of a low ridge that runs from the south-west to the north-east and a walled fortification surround them. The city and the palace together are approximately ten kilometres in circumference covering the narrow top of the ridge and seem like an imperial camp frozen in stone. And according to S. A. A. Rizvi, it 'was designed to serve as the cultural, commercial and administrative centre of the empire; upon rebellion or invasion the Emperor and the Court could fall back to the strong fort of Agra.' The two earliest buildings here are the Stone Cutter's Mosque that the workers at the quarries built for Salim Chishti after he returned from a Haj in 1564 and the Rang Mahal that was built for Jodh Bai when the enceinte queen was sent to stay near the Sufi saint.

As Abul Fazl says, 'An order was issued that the superintendent of affairs should erect lofty buildings for the special use of the Shahinshah.' Akbar's personal world was designed around three connected rectangular courtyards and can be divided into three main areas—one the male domain or *mardana*, one the female quarters or the *zenana* and finally the area that was open to the public. The *mardana* area was called the Daulat Khana-i-Khas and the harem was the Haramsara. Then Abul Fazl goes on, 'In a short time there was a great city, and there were charming palaces. Benevolent institutions such as *khanquas* (seminaries), schools and baths, were also constructed, and a large stone bazaar was built. Beautiful gardens were made in the vicinity. A place of great concourse was brought together such as might move the envy of the world.'

The area open to the public included the caravanserai and the palace for public audiences, the Diwan-i-Aam. Then the area where the king lived and worked called the Daulat Khana-i-Khas and that included the palace of private audiences the Diwan-i-Khas, the treasury, his personal living quarters and the important office buildings nearby. Finally there was the secluded world of the Haramsara that was designed as a completely self-contained world with palaces, quarters of servants, gardens, kitchens and baths. They are all within walking distance of the king's residence called the Khwabgah that stands at one end of the main and largest courtyard.

> 4,441 cavalrymen, 10,717 horses, 12,000 musketeers, 5,000 women in the harem, 1,000 doorkeeper, 1,000 personal attendants, 6,000 elephants, 6,223 camels, 7,000 oxen, 260 mules, 5,000 deer, 1,000 cheetahs, plus craftsmen, building workers, couriers, clerks, painters and musicians.
>
> *A list of Akbar's personal expenses.*

Fatehpur Complex

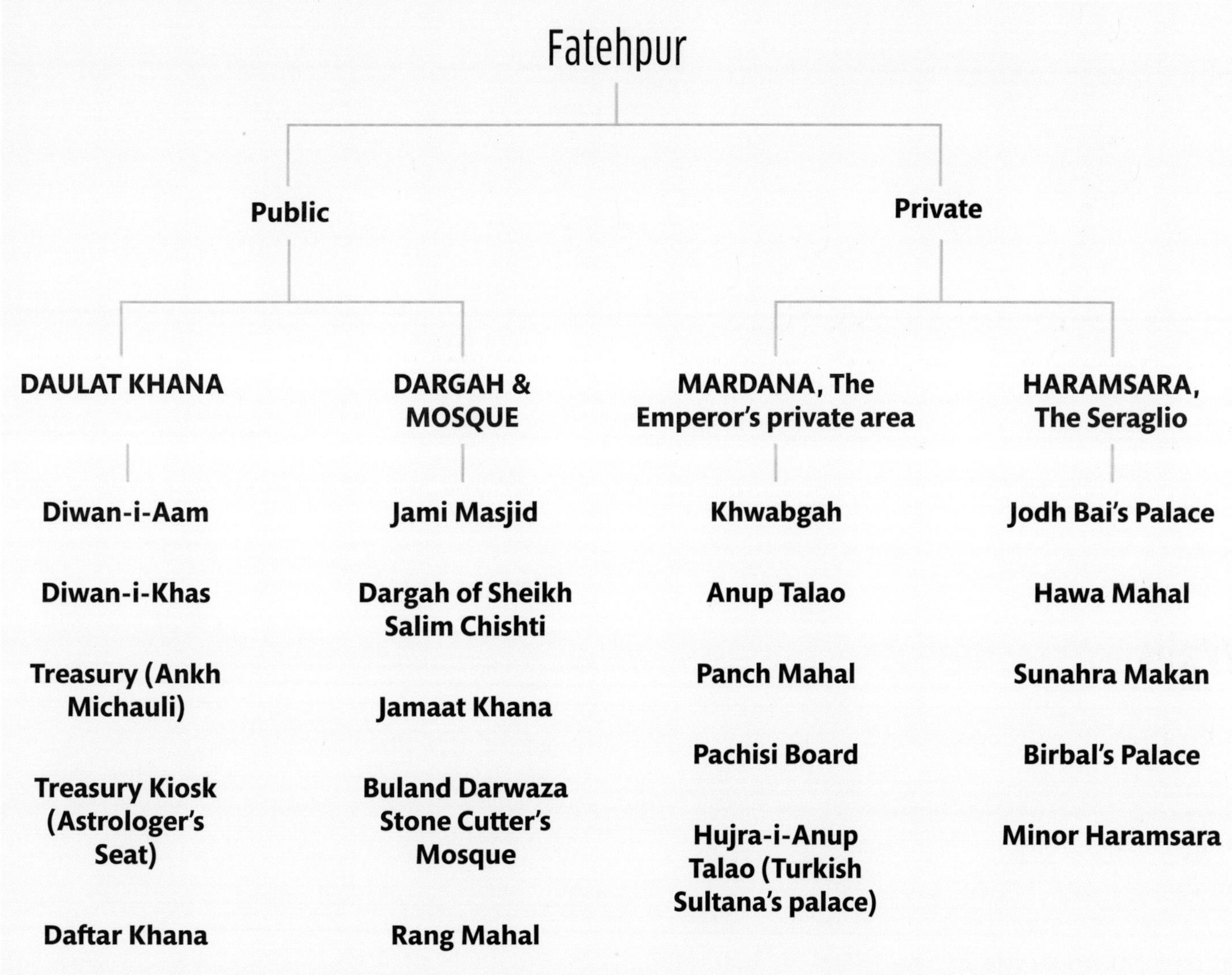

▲ A view of the Jami Masjid. Pilgrims enter the courtyard of the mosque to offer prayers.

▲ Gateways. The walls of the city had nine gateways including the famous Hathi Pol used by Akbar.

Walls and Gates

In medieval times all towns were surrounded by protective walls and here too a high stone wall with battlements and bastions, made of rubble with a stone facing, of close to six kilometres in length surrounds the palace complex. There are the typical loopholes on top and there is a wide path built inside from where the archers and matchlock-men could take aim and the guards marched up and down during their sentry duty. The walls were built on three sides of the city with the fourth protected by the lake on which Akbar built the Terah Mori or Thirteen Gates Dam. Compared to the high, thick walls, embattlements and bastions of the Agra Fort these walls here are of little military value and in case of any threat, as at the time when Salim began to rebel, Akbar would have had to retreat to his old fortress.

The walls are pierced by nine gateways that opened on to roads that lead to important cities like Delhi and Lahore and are named after them. The gates are nearly identical in design with semi-circular bastions flanking the entrance and two tiers

▲ *Walls. Unlike the high ramparts and bastions of the Agra Fort here the walls are low and have simple battlements.*

▲ *The Buland Darwaza was a later addition to the complex of the mosque.*

of loopholes on top. Most visitors will approach the palaces through the Agra Gate that was called the Akbarabad Gate during Akbar's reign. As you enter through this gate, on the right is an enclosure with ruined cloisters that was once a famous caravanserai. It is just a pile of rubble now but was still standing in 1610 when William Finch came here and wrote, 'Close within the gate is the King's Saray, with large stone lodgings but much ruined.'

Then the road goes under a walled enclosure with three arches called the Naubat or Naqqar Khana. This was where the drums boomed out as the imperial band greeted the arrival of the king in the Diwan-i-Aam and also marked the passing of hours. There is another Naubat Khana above the Hathi Pol as Akbar often used that gateway to enter the city and it has images of two elephants flanking the gate and it was often shown in miniature paintings. The other gates are the Delhi Darwaza in Sikri village, also the gates named Lal (red), Suraj (sun), Chander (moon) and the Gwalior and Ajmeri darwazas and one amusingly dubbed Terha Darwaza or the crooked gate.

Diwan-i-Aam

The first important palace that visitors encounter on entering the royal enclosure is Akbar's palace of public audiences, the Diwan-i-Aam, at times also called the Diwankhana-i-Aam. This was an important building, the only one that most people had the good fortune to see. During his reign this is where the common citizen would have ended his journey as beyond it was the guarded domain of the king. One walks though a high square doorway and it opens out into an expansive courtyard of green lawns and flower beds surrounded by a colonnaded corridor. Akbar was very particular about being accessible to his subjects and this is where the people came every day to petition the king during regular gatherings of citizens and nobility.

The Diwan-i-Aam is a red sandstone rectangular pavilion with a flat, sloping roof. In front there are five alcoves divided by columns topped by corbels jutting out to support the roof and the overhanging eaves called *chhajas*. Every day, three hours after sunrise, Akbar left his residence, and immediately the drums began to play over the Naubat Khana. People would be waiting before the royal seat and the gathering would stand up and bow in the low kornish and the royal audience would begin. The king sat on his bejewelled throne

◄ *Diwan-i-Aam. The hall of public audience was where a Mughal king listened to petitions of his subjects and dispensed justice.*

in the central bay that must have been luxuriously furnished with soft Persian carpets strewn with large silk bolsters and to create a private space there are screens on both sides intricately carved in geometric patterns. His senior ministers would occupy the enclosures on both sides.

Before him, around the courtyard, would be a crowd of people rich and poor, mostly men and a few women, who were a cross section of his subjects. Here every morning he listened to his people and dispensed justice in criminal cases. Monserrate comments on how he listened patiently to even the poorest of his subjects and passed judgement sternly but with fairness and impartiality. A couple of executioners would stand nearby holding instruments of torture but they were only there to instil fear in people and no executions were carried out here. In the afternoons Akbar would come to the Diwan-i-Aam again to inspect the horses and elephants from the royal stables and also meet officials to manage the administrative work of the empire. The tourist guides will point to the great stone rings at the foot of the colonnades right across from the royal pavilion and say that elephants were tied here and they were used to crush criminals under their feet. In fact, Akbar was never known to use such barbaric methods of public execution. He had a special love for elephants, and had his favourite animals, all richly caparisoned, standing there before him to add a touch of glamour to the occasion.

▶ *Diwan-i-Khas. Some historians feel this was a part of the treasury and held the royal jewels.*

Diwan-i-Khas

A door at the back of the Diwan-i-Aam leads into the mardana area of the fortress. This was the daily route that Akbar took to go to the next walled courtyard where his main palaces stood. And the most interesting is the oddly enigmatic palace called the Diwan-i-Khas, or the hall of private audience that is also at times called the Jewel House. It is a pretty square palace with four kiosks, the *chhatris*, placed in the corners of the roof. From outside the Diwan-i-Khas looks like a two storied palace with doorways opening out into a balcony on the first floor but in fact the inside has a surprise for the visitor.

The palace is one high ceilinged chamber and in the middle there is an astonishing stone pillar topped by a circular seat. It creates an ambience like no palace anywhere in the world and the design

'The fact that Akbar married a number of Rajput princesses and that he granted Amritsar as a fief to the Sikh leader Ramdas, had political rather than religious reasons, and his interest in the Jesuit fathers sprang from his insatiable curiosity. It seems that the "un-Islamic" trends in Akbar's politics have also been exaggerated by the Jesuits who had hoped to win him over to Christianity.'

***Annemarie Schimmel** on Akbar's religious policy.*

was not repeated by any later Mughal ruler. It also puzzles the visitor because it is very hard to fathom the purpose of the strange construction. The stone capital, thick as a tree trunk, is richly carved in an intricate maze of floral and geometric patterns. It is square at the base, then octagonal and then dividing further into sixteen sides. Finally it opens out like a flower on top in rows of thirty-six serpentine brackets that support a round platform seat surrounded by a low screened balcony. From this seat, narrow stone walkways connect it to semi-circular galleries in the corners of the room and these can be reached by staircases built into the walls.

One stands there in the red gold gloom staring upwards in bemusement, wondering what Akbar could possibly have done here. One can write a small book about the various speculations by archaeologist, historians and visitors about the purpose of this palace—private audiences, inspecting the royal jewels, meeting of religious leaders or declaring his new religion, the Din-i-Ilahi. Also one would have thought that such an unusual design would have been described by the royal historians, oddly enough, none of them do so.

Traditionally, a Diwan-i-Khas was the palace where a king carried on the business of the empire. He met officials, heard reports from the provinces and important visitors from foreign lands, royal envoys and travellers came to pay their respects. It is hard to imagine how the king could have functioned

◀ *Diwan-i-Khas. The extraordinary pillar that stands in the centre of the room with a circular seat on top.*

because he would be sitting halfway up in the air with some people crowded into the corner galleries and the rest gathered below. It is not possible that a practical and enterprising king like Akbar would have planned anything so awkward. The problem is that no contemporary writer talks about the purpose of the building, leaving us to the pleasures of wildly imaginative speculation.

The whole design is intriguing but it is not beautiful and the pillar will remain an enigma forever. Some historians feel this pillar was the Satun-i-Adl or the column of justice and Akbar announced important decisions from the top. Some think it is

▼ *The pillar has a square base that becomes octagonal and then divides into sixteen sides.*

a version of the Hindu mandala and the seat was used for ritualistic purposes like annual religious festivals with the king being placed in the centre of his universe. Others speculate that it was the Ibadat Khana where Akbar met philosophers and religious teachers for discussion but many think that such a palace would have been near the Jami Masjid and not within the official area. Rizvi in the handbook of the Archaeological Survey of India calls it the Jewel House where the royal treasures were stored. Abul Fazl wrote that there were three separate treasuries, one for copper coins, the second for gold and silver coins and one for gems and jewels and Rizvi imagines Akbar sitting on the platform, 'suspended in the air' inspecting his jewels like a connoisseur.

Ankh Michauli

The word *ankh michauli* means blind man's buff in Hindi and if ever a palace was absurdly named by romantic tourist guides it is this one. The pavilion stands right next to the Diwan-i-Khas in the main court of the king where all the important work of the empire was carried out. And here the guides will tell you that Akbar played a childish game with his queens! Rizvi says with severe disapproval of such frivolous suggestions, 'There is small possibility of truth in this.' Even though no one believes it, the utterly inappropriate but oddly beguiling name has stuck.

◀ *Treasury. Imaginatively called Ankh Michauli, the palace for playing blind man's buff.*

As Rizvi comments, 'of the institutions of the central government, the most important were the imperial treasures. Akbar bestowed his personal attention upon their management and looked after the administration of revenue and public expenditure with great care.' So it would be practical to have his main treasury or Khazana next to his audience hall in the main Daulat Khana quadrangle. There was also another larger building nearby that collapsed in 1892 that had been the treasury for copper coins. So study this pavilion as a treasury where the huge treasury of gold and silver coins was stored. Look up at the serpentine struts resting on corbels that project from the walls. Each is shaped like a mythical monster with an open mouth out of which an inscribed scroll emerges and these serpent monsters have been the traditional guards of treasuries in India. The doors are made of stone and all along the wall there are recessed spaces with sliding slabs on top where the gold and silver coins must have been stored.

'The magnificent architectural heritage of Samarkand, Herat, and other Timurid cities played a major role in the development of the Mughal architectural tradition.'

***Catherine B. Asher** on the architecture of Fatehpur Sikri.*

The Treasury Kiosk

Right before the Treasury is an open, elaborately decorated kiosk that is traditionally called the Astrologer's Seat. If you ask the tourist guides, what an astrologer was doing sitting outside a palace where the king was flirting with the harem ladies, you will of course not get an answer! Also no contemporary chronicle mentions any astrologer who was so powerful that he would be assigned a separate seat in the Daulat Khana. Akbar did believe in predictions but preferred to consult a team of astrologers from various schools. Logically this kiosk would be the seat where an important revenue official or even Akbar himself sat while supervising the working of the treasury.

It is like many kiosks that one finds among the palaces but what places it apart is the way it is ornamented by serpentine stone brackets in each corner, creating a seat of importance. The brackets are similar to the torana carvings that can be seen in the temples of Gujarat. Monserrate describes how copper coins were heaped in the courtyard to be distributed as salary to officials and servants and for charity. So it also possible that the pavilion was occupied by the Chief Treasurer, a eunuch named Phul Malik who was given the title of Khwaja-sara Itimad Khan by Akbar. He would

◀ *Astrologer's Seat. No astrologer sat here. It was probably the seat of the head of the treasury.*

sit here and supervise the complex work of payments and expenditure.

▲ *Toran. Akbar's conquest of Gujarat led to the arrival of Gujarati craftsmen who used this traditional design.*

Panch Mahal and Pachisi Board

Standing at the door of the Diwan-i-Khas one is faced by the open expanse of a huge stone court with rows of cloisters and palaces surrounding it. On the right is an airy, five-storey structure called the Panch Mahal and once again you wonder why this design was chosen. What was the purpose of the building? It is open on all sides and made entirely of columns with the four upper stories supported by a total of eighty-four pillars, the first with fifty-six, the second by twenty, the third by twelve and the upper most floor, which is a single domed kiosk, by four pillars. But it is not a pyramidal shape, instead the storeys are reduced towards the south only, creating a slope like a hill.

Archaeologists think this was a palace called a badgir or the Wind Tower, and as it stands right at the edge of the *zenana* and *mardana* areas, it probably was where the king and harem ladies came to enjoy the breeze in the summer. One can look straight into the main harem palaces from the top so it is certain that only the royal family would have had to access to this tower. Akbar may also have climbed to the top to survey the city and during his time there were carved screens connecting the pillars that would have created the privacy required by the ladies. These screens were removed in the nineteenth century by

▶ *Panch Mahal. In Akbar's time carved screens would have hidden the royal women from view.*

the British. No two pillars are exactly identical; some are circular and others octagonal and they are covered in patterns of vases of flowers, bells and chains and topped by intricately carved lintels. One has to move carefully, climbing to the other floors as the steps are very high and at times without comfortable handholds. However the precarious climb is worth the effort because from the top, one catches an unparalleled vista of Fatehpur Sikri. A panorama of all the palaces of the Daulat Khana and the Haramsara, the nameless pavilions and ruined barracks in the outskirts and far beyond at the horizon, the stretches of fields that was the site of the lake. In the courtyard right in front is an inlaid marble pattern on the floor that resembles a *pachisi* board placed before a small platform. A fanciful explanation is that Akbar played *pachisi* here using women as living pieces. Akbar did enjoy the game but

▼ *Panch Mahal. The palace is topped with a single four pillared kiosk.*

oddly enough no contemporary chronicle mentions him playing with living pieces and it would have been worth writing about. Some later Mughal kings did stay for short periods of time at Fatehpur Sikri including Jahangir and Mohammad Shah and it is possible that the *pachisi* board may have been laid by one of them.

▼ *Pachisi Board. It is not mentioned by any contemporary historian and was probably added by a later king.*

'Most of the credit must be given to Akbar's extra-ordinary personal gifts as a ruler, organizer, and commander of men. He gathered trusted confidants around him whose abilities nearly matched his own. He was, however, his own strategist and executive officer who vigorously commanded his armies in the field.'

***John F. Richards** on Akbar, the empire builder.*

Anup Talao

It is called the 'Peerless Pool' and both Monserrate and Jahangir refer to it as the Kapur Talao. Completed in 1575, it is a delightful square tank placed right before Akbar's residence, the Khwabgah. In the centre is a square stone seat that is connected to the sides by narrow walkways and it echoes the plan of a central seat and connecting passages that we see inside the Diwan-i-Aam. Legend has it that Mian Tansen, Akbar's famous court singer used to stand here and serenade his monarch with his music. Standing in the centre of the pool, one can imagine the dazzling spectacle of a night concert here, with the omrahs gathered round the pool and the harem ladies sitting behind woven chik curtains. As the tall lamps glowed in the dark and the air was redolent with the aroma of flowers and incense; in the centre Tansen singing one of his melodious ragas—Mian ki Malhar or Darbari Kanada as small earthen lamps floated in the water of the ornamental pool as if reflecting the starry skies above.

According to Jahangir, in 1578 while hunting in the forests of Punjab his father had a mystical vision which made him cancel the hunt and release all the animals that had been corralled for slaughter. On his return he had the Anup Talao filled with mostly copper but also some gold and silver coins worth over a crore of rupees and he distributed these to his subjects so that 'the general public might receive an abundant share of the sublime beauty'.

◀ *Anup Talao. The square pool with a seat in the centre is the visual symbol of the city.*

▲ *Anup Talao. Tradition says that the legendary Mian Tansen sang here for his king.*

And then Jahangir adds with a touch of irony, 'For a long time the thirsty-lipped ones of the desert of desire were satisfied from the fountain of benignity.'

Khwabgah

Khwabgah means the 'house of dreams' and the two storeyed building standing right next to the Anup Talao was probably the personal palace and bed chamber of the king. The Khwabgah, also called the Khilwatkada-i-Khas occupies the whole southern half of the mardana court and the king may have used it not just as a bedroom but also for confidential meetings. At one time these rooms were not just ornamented by carvings but also the walls were covered by brightly coloured murals. If you look carefully you can still see faint traces of the drawings of tulips, poppies and roses. Here, every night Akbar

▶ *Khwabgah. Called the Palace of Dreams, it was Akbar's personal domain.*

► *A panoramic view captures the expanse of the Daulat Khana-i-Khas.*

had books read out to him. There is a possibility that may be they were stored in the wall openings that are covered by sliding stone slabs. There is a larger room with a platform that Monserrate describes as being covered in silk carpets and strewn with bolsters and cushions to create 'a couch covered with scarlet rugs' where the king reclined as he met officials and visitors.

Akbar's bedroom or the real palace of dreams was an ornamental chamber on the first floor and this was connected to the harem by a covered passage and here the queens and concubines spent time with him. In these rooms Akbar would also have relaxed in the company of close friends like Abul Fazl and Raja Birbal, after the long and strenuous sessions at the audiences. He was a convivial man who enjoyed being surrounded by people and would summon interesting men to entertain him and one of them met him at his window. There is a window set high on one wall from where Akbar showed himself every day to his subjects in the ceremony that he devised called Jharokha-i-Darshan. This window seemed to have been Akbar's window to the world because Badauni writes that a Brahmin named Devi, who was a scholar of the *Mahabharata*, would be pulled up sitting on a string bed till he was level with the *jharokha* and hanging in mid air he had long discussions with the king about Hinduism. Also at times the area before the Anup Talao used to be closed off with a canvas screen so that Akbar and his ministers could say their prayers there.

Turkish Sultana's Palace

At the north-east corner of the Anup Talao is a jewel-like pavilion that is often called the Turkish Sultana's palace, supposedly the residence of an unnamed Turkish queen. Historians point out that this palace is in the mardana area where a queen would never be allowed to live. Also it is clearly part of the complex meant for the personal use of the king. It is a square building that is connected to the Khwabgah by a colonnade, clearly meant for the passage of the king.

The palace is a delightful creation, designed like a village hut with low hanging eaves resembling a thatched roof and originally the portico and veranda were covered by lattice screens. Virtually every inch of the walls, roof and pillars are covered with carvings with the consistency of lace and it is the most ornamental of the palaces with pillars, pilasters and walls decorated in delicate floral, geometric and arabesques patterns that remind one of textile weaves. The interiors are also chiselled with scenes from nature and a tree of life with such fineness that it seems like the carvers were working with soft wood not stone. If this had been the residence of a queen, this mysterious Turkish Sultana would have been a very important personage indeed to live in the private court in such close proximity to the monarch. However no contemporary historian mentions anyone by that title. The palace was clearly a place of repose attached to

▶ *Turkish Sultana's Palace. It has a roof carved to resemble a wooden hut.*

the Anup Talao used by the king to relax and Badauni does mention a palace called the Hujra-i-Anup Talao.

Turkish Sultana's Palace

In contemporary chronicles this palace was called Hujra-i-Anup Talao. Akbar used it to meet people and no mysterious Turkish queen lived here.

Daftar Khana

The Record Room or Daftar Khana stands at one end of the main enclosure, close to the Khwabgah. Built much later than the other buildings, in 1574-75, it has a platform supported by piers and arches and the northern facade has six pairs of double columns with bracketed capitals and overhanging eaves. These are ornamented by intricate carvings and with interesting bases in a pyramidal shape and scalloped

▼ *A variety of designs used to decorate the stone including geometric patterns, grape vines, flowers and stars.*

▼ *An Islamic geometric pattern often used in screens.*

and chiselled with the pattern of a peacock's tail. Akbar's translation bureau, the Maktab Khana also stood nearby where classics of other languages were translated but the building has vanished.

Akbar's new religious creed Din-i-Ilahi was also called Tauhid-i-Ilahi. Akbar imagined it as an order of brotherhood rather than a new religion.

▼ A rare use of grapes and vines as a carving was a sign of coming together of various traditions under Akbar.

▼ A compilation of typical geometric designs of Islamic influence with the inverted lotus which was predominantly a Hindu motif.

▲ *Haramsara. The niches in the walls may have been used to place lamps.*

THE HARAMSARA

The Royal Seraglio

In every Mughal fortress the imperial harem takes up a large space. The Haramsara was the area where the royal women—queens, princesses and concubines

▲ *Haramsara. The interiors would have been covered in carpets and luxurious furnishings.*

lived and it was kept secluded behind walls, screens, garden hedges and was very well guarded. For a monarch the seraglio was among the most important institutions of the state and some of the women played a significant role in the work of the empire. The senior most member of the haramsara, in Akbar's case his mother Hamida Bano Begum, managed an establishment of hundreds of women. She was also the guardian of the two seals of the realm that were used to stamp all the royal orders or *firmans*. The king spent a part of each day here supervising

its administration and often had a meal here. The opening to the Haramsara area is from the Khwabgah side and is separated by a row of cloisters. It was guarded very well according to Abul Fazl, 'The inside of the Harem is guarded by senior and active women ... outside of the enclosure the eunuchs are placed; and at a proper distance, there is a guard of faithful Rajputs, beyond whom are the porters of the gates. Besides, on all four sides, there are guards of nobles, ahadis, and other troops.'

There has been much speculation about the number of wives that Akbar married and gossip

credits him with a Portuguese Christian and a Turkish wife. With his usual hyperbole Abul Fazl declares that Akbar had 5,000 women in the harem but looking at the area assigned to it at Fatehpur Sikri, it is hard to imagine such a number being accommodated here. Monserrate says, 'Zelaldinus (Jalaluddin) has more than three hundred wives dwelling in separate suites of rooms in a very large palace.' The women who gained prominence during the years at Fatehpur Sikri

▲ *Haramsara. Akbar's Rajput queens including Mariam-us-Zamani lived in rooms around this courtyard.*

included the Queen Mother Hamida Bano who had the title Mariam Makani (equal in rank to Mary), his aunt Gulbadan, his two senior wives Salima Sultan Begum and Ruquaiya Begum. The youngest was his first Rajput queen, the mother of the heir-apparent, the princess of Amber who was given the title of Mariam-us-Zamani (the Mary of her age). Popular tradition calls her Jodh Bai but the royal chronicles only give her title.

Jodh Bai's Palace

This is the largest palace in the seraglio and it is connected to the Minor Haramsara quarters, baths and a garden. The Khwabgah was connected to this palace by a covered passage and at the left of the entrance is a small guardhouse where the Rajput guards would stay. Tradition says that Akbar's Rajput queens and the Hindu wives of Prince Salim lived here and were allowed to freely practise their religion. Tourist guides will point to a small stand in the middle of the courtyard and tell you that a sacred tulsi plant used in worship grew there. Abul Fazl says Akbar performed *homa*, the Hindu fire sacrifice here, that was bitterly condemned by the mullahs including Badauni. And it saw colourful celebrations during festivals like Deepavali and Dussehra with the king joining in with great enthusiasm.

◀ *Haramsara. Only the men of the royal family were permitted to enter the seraglio.*

From the outside the palace has a blank and rather forbidding look with a windowless, unbroken span of stone walls. The main entrance is double storeyed, projecting out of the facade to create a kind of porch leading into a recessed entrance with a balcony. The entrance passage turns right and opens out into an airy quadrangle surrounded by rooms that welcomes the visitor to an elegant and intimate feminine world. The columns of the rooms are all ornamented with carvings and start as four-sided at the bottom and ultimately have sixteen sides at the top like the ones at the Panch Mahal. The bases and capitals are ornamented with a variety of Hindu sculptural motifs—small lozenges, rosettes, lotuses and the popular bell and chain. A startling touch of colour is added by the tiled roofs of the northern and southern wings and you can see it from the

▼ *A variety of carved decorations seen all across the palaces.*

upper floors of the Panch Mahal and even catch a flash of blue from the top of the Buland Darwaza. The glazed tiles that came from Multan are an eye-catching shade of turquoise and even today give the palace a gentle exuberance in a pragmatic world of red sandstone.

Between Jodh Bai's Palace and Sunahra Makan stands a square building that has richly carved exterior walls that is often called Jodh Bai's Kitchen. Usually the building is locked but the walls are worth a close look as they are completely covered in pretty carving in a herring-bone patterns interspersed with rosettes. It is hard to imagine a queen being assigned such a large building as her kitchen and this was probably an office attached to the Haramsara.

Hawa Mahal

In the summer heat of North India, a hawa mahal, or palace of breezes, was often added to the harem. The Hawa Mahal at Fatehpur Sikri is a double storey extension at the back of the northern wing of Jodh Bai's Palace. The first storey is an open pillared hall and the second is screened for privacy and here the ladies could relax in seclusion as they enjoyed the vista and savoured the breeze. The Hawa Mahal is accessible from Jodh Bai's Palace and also through the zenana garden that once stood behind the building.

▶ *Haramsara. The arched niches in the walls can be seen in the private palaces.*

▲ *Sunahra Makan. The interiors were embellished with coloured tiles and calligraphy.*

Sunahra Makan

Right before Jodh Bai's palace is a pavilion called Sunahra Makan, the golden house and also Mariam ki Kothi. After telling you about a Turkish queen no one knew about, the tourist guides will now tell a fanciful tale of a Portuguese queen named Maria who lived here. This comes from people being unaware of the two Mariams who were living in Akbar's seraglio—his mother Mariam Makani and his wife Mariam-us-Zamani. The younger Mariam or Jodh Bai lived with the other Hindu queens in the main Haramsara quadrangle. This separate palace was for the head of the harem, the redoubtable and very influential Hamida Bano Begum or Mariam Makani who was her son's adviser and support till her death in 1603. Her closest friend was her sister-in-law Gulbadan Begum who was about her age, and it is possible she also lived here, thus providing a matriarchal enclave for the king.

This becomes even clearer if you study the layout of the harem area because the Sunahra Makan is the palace closest to Akbar's residence. The roof,

▲ *Sunahra Makan. The paintings on the walls have faded over the centuries.*

▲ *Sunahra Makan. In Akbar's time this was one of the most opoulently decorated palaces.*

with overhanging eaves, is supported by carved brackets and shows some intriguing carvings. One shows the Hindu god Rama being worshipped by his monkey acolyte Hanuman, and also a pair of geese and elephants. The inside walls were once painted in rich colours but have faded into faint tracery hard to decipher and the profuse use of gold leaf must have led to the naming of the palace as the sunahra (golden) makan (house). There is a Persian couplet reputed to have been composed by the poet laureate Faizi that is inscribed on the lintels supporting the ceiling and says,

'This building excels the seventh heaven in glory,
The excellence of the Kaba is beyond question,
But this mansion has a purity of its own.'

Birbal's Palace

Another palace with a completely inappropriate name is a double storey building near Jodh Bai's Palace said to be Birbal's Palace. The pavilion is in the heart of the Haramsara where only the male members of the royal family were allowed to enter. So it is impossible that Birbal would have been assigned a palace here. As a matter of fact all the courtiers built their mansions outside the walls including Todar Mal, Abdur Rahim and Abul Fazl. Birbal would have done the same. This palace was probably occupied by Akbar's two senior queens Salima Sultan Begum and Ruquaiya Begum. These two women were of royal lineage, both descendants

▶ *Birbal's Palace. As a part of the Haramsara it was in fact the residence of Akbar's queens.*

of Babur. Ruquaiya was the daughter of Akbar's uncle Mirza Hindal and Salima was the daughter of his aunt Gulrukh and they deserved a separate palace being assigned to them.

This is one of the most attractively designed palaces in the Haramsara. It is double storeyed with four large rooms on the ground floor. The two rooms on the second floor are placed corner to corner instead of beside each other, thus creating two private and shady terraces. The rooms are topped by double domes curving up to a finial. The walls have pilasters that are finely carved with recessed arches creating spaces like picture frames with rosettes and spandrels. The ornamental motifs are predominantly Hindu which may have led to the misconception that this was the residence of a Hindu courtier but this palace was definitely a part of the Haramsara.

▼ *Niche in the wall of the palace the purpose of which can only be guessed.*

▼ *Intricate carvings embellish a palace interior reflecting the finesse of the artisans.*

Minor Haramsara

At the back of Jodh Bai's Palace stand a curious row of rooms facing each other in a broad colonnade. It has been called a stable for horses, camels or the Filkhana, the stable for elephants mainly because of the layout of two rows of rooms. However it was clearly the residential rooms of other harem women. A noisy, smelly stable, where stable hands would be constantly going in and out, would never have been placed so close to the main Haramsara. The stone rings fitted to the bays would have been used to tie curtains and not animals. This space would have been more suitable as the quarters of less important harem ladies and the maids who served the royal women and there is a *hammam* nearby for their use. A road leads out of this building to one of the important gates of the city, the Hathi Pol.

▼ *Palace walls were given extra importance and were often decorated with delicate carvings.*

▼ *A lotus motif has been placed at the heart of the majorly geometrical pattern.*

A MATTER OF FAITH

A matter of faith

'The emperor turned more towards a mystical approach to religion, which was, after all, better suited to bring together the different peoples in his empire.'

-Annemarie Schimmel

The early Mughal rulers, especially Akbar, had an instinctive affinity to Sufism and its mystic search for truth. Babur, when he arrived in Delhi in 1526, first went to pray at all the Sufi shrines and Humayun's Tomb was built by Akbar at a site close to the dargah of Sheikh Nizamuddin Auliya. The open and mystical world of the Sufis with its emphasis on love and tolerance melded well with their liberal and aesthetic world view as most of the early Mughal rulers were not religious bigots. Akbar was genuinely curious about other religions and among all the myriad faiths that he explored at the discourses in his Ibadat Khana were not just the major religions of Islam, Christianity and Hinduism but also Zoroastrianism, Jainism and even atheism. However what stayed constant in his life was his interest in Sufism and the state religion that he created and named Din-i-Ilahi reflects the influence of Sufi thinkers like Abul Fazl's father, Sheikh Mubarak.

Suf means wool and refers to the rough woollen garments worn by the Sufi sages who chose an austere life of meditation and prayers. Sufism is the mystic stream of Islam that first appeared in the eighth century and at the heart of its system is the

◀ *Prayers at the hallowed shrine of Sheikh Salim Chishti.*

teacher-disciple—the *pir-murid* tradition, where the teacher is addressed as the Sheikh. The teachers use their knowledge of the Muslim holy books and also fables and parables to illustrate their beliefs, like the famous Mulla Nasruddin tales that use humour to make a philosophical point. Sufism strives for a mystical union of the individual soul into the Supreme Being through meditation and even sessions of devotional music called *sama* and ecstatic dance called *raqs*.

The shrines of Sufi saints are open to everybody and they welcome people of every faith. It is an ecstatic, mystical faith that moves with emotions and beliefs and as Idries Shah says gently, 'Sufism ... is not available on the basis of assumptions which belong to another world, the world of the intellect.' The tombs are filled with the faithful during the Urs festivals

▼ *The music of the quawwali singers echo across the courtyard.*

and sway in joyous praise of their beloved 'Khwaja' through music and prayers. It is a pantheistic faith that encourages personal devotion with the faithful seeking a direct and emotional communion with god that is in many ways very similar to the Hindu devotional beliefs of Bhakti. As Annemarie Schimmel comments, 'Islam in the subcontinent always displayed two faces which we might call, for want of a better term, the India-oriented "mystical" inclusive one and the Mecca-oriented "prophetic" exclusive one.'

Akbar often went to the dargahs of Sufi pirs like that of Muinuddin Chishti at Ajmer that he visited every year in the 1570s and 1580s. It was while returning from a trip to Ajmer that he stopped at the seminary, the *khanqua*, of a living pir, Sheikh Salim Chishti at the village of Sikri. The village people told him about this recluse who lived in a hut on

▼ *A ceremonial chadar of thanksgiving being presented at the Dargah of Sheikh Muinuddin Chishti at Ajmer.*

▲ *Travelling Sufis and praying women gather at the doors of the dargah at Ajmer.*

▲ *Pilgrims belonging to many religions visit the Sufi shrines to pray and make a wish.*

▲ *Trditional rituals of prayer at the dargah. Sufi dargahs are open to people from all faiths.*

top of the hill and this meeting gave a wonderful turn to Akbar's life. The king believed that it was Salim Chishti's blessings that led to the birth of the three sons who grew to maturity and thus saved the future of the dynasty. After that the Sufi saint's sacred presence became essential to Akbar especially when he undertook the ambitious plans of building a new city.

Salim Chishti and the Chishtiya Order

There are a number of Sufi schools that have existed in India from the thirteenth century and the most influential are the Chishtis. There are three other important Sufi orders in India, the wandering dervishes called Qalandars, the Suhrawardis and the Naqshbandis but it is the Chishti order or *silsila* that gained the most popularity among the common people of the land. The order is named after a place in Syria where it began and the first Chishti pir to arrive in India in the wake of the invasions of Mahmud of Ghazni was Muinuddin Chishti. He established a seminary or *khanqua* in Ajmer in Rajasthan in the thirteenth century and even today the shrine or dargah of the 'Garib Nawaz' or the protector of the poor is the most popular Sufi pilgrimage for believers. A number of other Chishti preachers followed, like Qutubuddin Bakhtiar Kaki, Fariduddin Ganj-i-Shakar and Nizamuddin Auliya. They all lived in Delhi and were influential preachers during the Sultanate period.

◀ *For Akbar the Dargah of Salim Chishti was the spiritual heart of his empire.*

▲ *The grave of Salim Chishti is covered by an ornamental canopy covered in mother of pearl.*

The tombs or *mazhar*s of these spiritual preceptors have become pilgrimages for people of every faith and illustrate how kings come and go but a great teacher lives on in the hearts of the people. One story that people have never forgotten is about the conflict that took place in Delhi between Sultan Ghiyasuddin Tughlak and Nizamuddin Auliya. The sultan was building his fortress and did not like the workers building a *baoli*, a water tank, for the pir and tried his best to stop it. He failed, and today Tughlakabad is a desolate ruin while the dargah at Nizamuddin Basti is alive with pilgrims and echoing to prayers and songs composed by the pir's greatest disciple, the poet Amir Khusro.

The life of a Sufi pir was an enigma. They spent it within society, most of them married and had children but still they remained outside social mores, living a reclusive life of meditation and poverty. They were practising Muslims but did not ask the faith of their followers as every one was welcome in their seminaries and Chishti saints were known to hold discussions with Hindu yogis. They acted as preachers and counsellors to their followers as they were well educated in Muslim theology. All the donations they received were distributed among the poor and they lived by a vow of poverty. Their possessions make a spartan list very similar to the possessions allowed by the Buddha for the monks of the Sangha. All that the Sufi wanderer carried with him was a copy of the Quran, a staff, a prayer carpet, a robe, a begging bowl, a turban and a rosary.

Sheikh Salim Chishti lived the life of a Sufi preacher in the same tradition as all the other pirs who had come before him. He was the descendant of the saint Fariduddin Ganj-e-Shakar of Pak Pattan in Pakistan. He was born in 1480 at Delhi but the family shifted to Sikri soon after. He was in his forties when he left on his first pilgrimage to Mecca and came back a decade later. Soon his piety had won him many followers and among them were the stonecutters who were quarrying the red sandstone of the Sikri ridge for the fortress that Akbar was building at Agra. They built a mosque for him which is now called the Stone Cutter's Mosque and this was the first building to come up on the ridge at Sikri. When the princess of Amber became pregnant she was shifted to live near the saint and a small palace,

Ajmer Sharif

In the thirteenth century the Sufi saint Sheikh Muinuddin Chishti arrived in India. He was the first preacher of the Sufi Chishtiya order to establish a seminary here and his dargah at Ajmer is the oldest in the country. He is called 'Garib Nawaaz', a friend of the poor, by his devotees. Among the later Sufi pirs are Sheikh Qutubuddin Bakhtiar Kaki, Sheikh Fariduddin Ganj-i-Shakar, Sheikh Nizamuddin Auliya and Sheikh Salim Chishti of Fatehpur Sikri belongs to the same order.

▼ *Pilgrims participating by offering prayers and singing at the dargah during the festival of Urs.*

Rang Mahal was built for her. The actual building of the citadel would start three years later.

When Akbar met him in 1568 the Sufi sage was in his late eighties. The birth of three sons—Salim, Murad and Daniyal made him the pre-eminent saint for Akbar and he gave him the title of Sheikh-ul-Islam. Salim Chishti lived long enough to see the Jami Masjid being built near his seminary and it was nearly complete when he died in 1572 at the age of ninety-two. The grieving emperor placed the tomb of his spiritual mentor in the middle of the courtyard of the mosque, where it still attracts thousands of pilgrims to his grave. Akbar made sure that Sheikh Salim Chishti was never forgotten by building a resting place that has the beauty of a jewel box and the welcoming ambience of a gentle, humane faith.

The Jami Masjid

The Jami Masjid or Great Mosque occupies the highest point of the Sikri ridge and its great gateway, the Buland Darwaza dominates the landscape with an arrogance that is oddly at variance with the elegant and welcoming shrine standing in its shadow. This was the main congregational mosque for Fatehpur and Badauni writes that it took five years to build and at that time it was the largest mosque in Hindustan. A chronogram is inscribed on the central archway composed by Ashraf Khan, one

▶ *Jami Masjid. Arched recesses called mihrabs mark the qibla, the direction towards Mecca.*

of Akbar's principal secretaries that reads,

'In the reign of the King of the world Akbar,
To whom is due the order in the country.
The Sheikh-ul-Islam adorned the mosque,
Which for its elegance deserves as much
reverence as the Ka'ba.
The year of the completion of this magnificent edifice,
Is found in the words, "duplicate of the Masjidi'l-Haram".'

Walking from the royal enclave one enters the Jami Masjid through the eastern gateway called the Badshahi Darwaza that faces the road from Agra. It is called the King's Gate as this was the doorway used by Badshah Akbar when he walked across from his palace to join the prayers. One walks up a flight of steps to reach a half hexagonal porch with an arched entrance. The gateway opens out into the wide expanse of the *sahn* or the mosque courtyard, and in the centre, in the shadow of a tree, is the mosque tank used for ablutions by the faithful before prayers. A new pavement was laid around the pool in 1743 under the supervision of Ghasi of Delhi and Mul Chand of Agra, both Hindus.

Right across the quadrangle is the main arch of the central prayer chamber and to the left the soaring gateway of the Buland Darwaza. To the right is the mausoleum of Salim Chishti, its pale marble gleaming in a framework of red sandstone. In his memoirs Jahangir writes that during holy occasions

◀ *Delicately carved geometrical patterns inlaid in marble.*

▲ *At Fatehpur Sikri the trabeate beam and lintel are seen more often than the Islamic arch.*

the kiosks placed along the top of the roof were covered in coloured cloth and rows of lamps were lit inside. In 1579 after Akbar had unveiled his new faith Din-i-Ilahi, he decided to read the Friday sermon here that deeply angered the orthodox Muslims.

Inside the mosque the arched recesses called *mihrab*s, mark the qibla, the direction to Mecca which Muslims face during prayers. In the three wings of the main prayer chamber there are three *mihrab*s in each of the seven bays and the central one is a pentagon topped by a semi dome and richly decorated with carvings of Quranic verses. Some of the *mihrab*s are ornamented with marble and glazed tiles in turquoise, green and white. The pulpit is to the right of the *mihrab* and it is a simple seat raised by three steps. It is from here that the Friday oration, the *khutba* was made in which there were prayers for

the welfare of the reigning monarch. The pillars running through the hallway are designed in the Hindu manner with a square section at the bottom becoming octagonal in the centre and then sixteen sided on the top. This was a style used by Indian craftsmen, especially from Gujarat and Akbar had brought many stone carvers from there. As S. A. A. Rizvi writes, 'This deliberate use of Hindu structural forms in a mosque had not been paralleled in northern India for well over three hundred years, since the first days of the Muslim conquest produced such pillared structures ... built of material plundered from Hindu temples.' This was different, as Akbar was deliberately choosing to use indigenous motifs within his mosque, thus creating a genuine synthesis that reflected the spirit of the people of his empire.

Sheikh Salim Chishti's Tomb

At the heart of the great congregational mosque, in the middle of the courtyard, stands the marble mausoleum of Sheikh Salim Chishti with an air of quiet serenity. This exquisite monument captures the imagination of every visitor and deserves every accolade showered on it. As Rizvi writes, 'it has often been described in superlatives; nothing else could capture its lyrical and enchanting beauty. It is, justly, one of the most famous examples of marble-work in India; it is also one of

◄ *Pilgrims from all across the land gather in a vibrant and colourful celebration of an inclusive faith.*

the finest.' It is completely made of marble like the Taj Mahal and the Itmad-ud-Daulah's tomb that one can see in Agra and both of them are stunningly beautiful. What makes this small tomb stand apart is in the restrained elegance of its adornments that is not trying to impress the viewer but instead filling their mind with peace. It is, as a true Sufi dargah, a gentle and welcoming place.

Salim Chishti originally had his seminary near the Stone Cutter's Mosque but then shifted to the north of the quadrangle of the Jami Masjid. The tomb was built at the place where he lived in a small cell and a small mosaic on the floor marks the spot where he used to say his prayers. The tomb was completed in 1581 and it was originally built in a mix of marble and sandstone, with the veranda and dome in red

▼ *A view through the intricate carved screens at the dargah.*

▶ *The eye-catching serpentine brackets at the entrance of the dargah.*

◀ *The dappled light and shadow of the ambulatory passage of the dargah.*

sandstone. Jahangir writes that his foster brother Qutbuddin Khan Koka added the marble screens that go round the veranda. There are no records of who added the marble eaves and the eye-catching serpentine brackets that hold them up. The dome was covered in marble as late as 1866 during British times when the magistrate of Agra got them veneered from the funds of the mausoleum.

The undulating stone brackets are the first thing a visitor notices, similar brackets can be seen in a simpler shape in the Stone Cutter's Mosque in red sandstone. Then as one steps inside the ambulatory passage one walks in the dappled light

▼ *Every screen is a marvellous blend of many sculptural designs.*

▼ *Close up of a carved marble border of the dargah of Salim Chishti.*

and shade cast by the utterly beautiful perforated screens. Study the many interlocking designs carved with such intricacy that the marble has been given the consistency of lace. There are stars, hexagons, triangles and just about every known geometric motif has been incorporated in a maze of delicate balance and symmetry. One can spend a long time while just strolling around the veranda admiring the magical work of Indian craftsmen. As John Lall writes, 'In life, Akbar honoured him with a city. In death, he offered the tribute of an exquisite casket as a tomb ... Emperor Jahangir further embellished it with marble carvings of exceptional delicacy.'

One enters the tomb chamber through an arched doorway and on top are carved the names of god, the Prophet and the four Caliphs, flanked by

▼ *The walls are brightened by red, black and ochre inlay work.*

▼ *The famous serpentine brackets of the dargah of Salim Chishti.*

painted flowers. Inside, the air is redolent with the fragrance of incense and the cenotaph is covered in a silk cover and always loaded with flowers. Above the cenotaph is a lovely wooden domed catafalque and it is covered in glistening mother-of-pearl. Here in an echo of Akbar's prayers, childless women of every faith come to pray for children. Tradition says that the faithful tie a thread on the screen when they ask for any blessing of the saint and then come back to untie it when their prayers have been answered.

Next to the shrine is a red sandstone, domed building which is called the Jamaat Khana where during the lifetime of the saint his disciples used to stay. Later it became the spot where members of the saint's family and his important disciples were buried. Among them was his grandson Islam Khan who rose to a high position in the Mughal bureaucracy. Next to it are rooms called the Zenana Rauza or women's tombs, where the saint used to meet people while the mosque was being built. Now it has many graves

◀ *Members of the family of Salim Chishti are buried around the dargah.*

▼ *Jami Masjid. Instead of minarets, the dome is surrounded by a row of chhatris.*

but during the time of Salim Chishti this was the spot where Akbar would join the saint at sessions of mystic music called the *sama*.

Buland Darwaza

At the opposite end of the court looms the massive gateway called the Buland Darwaza. Approaching it from outside one has to go up a long flight of steps to reach the giant archway. There is a message on the facade in delicate calligraphy that reads, 'Jesus, son of Mary (on whom be peace) said: the world is a bridge, pass over it but build no house upon it. Who hopes for an hour, hopes for eternity. The world is an hour, spend it in prayer, for the rest is unseen.'

The Buland Darwaza was not a part of the original design of the mosque. It was built to celebrate Akbar's conquest of Gujarat in 1573. It

was a campaign where he used a corps of camels to start a lightning strike on the army of the Sultan of Gujarat and won a tremendous victory in a campaign that took just eleven days. This meant that now the Mughals had access to the important ports of the Arabian Sea like Surat and Bharoach and the trade with the Gulf and further to Europe. This conquest would ultimately lead to the wealth of the Mughals growing so fast that they had to set up a mint at Surat to manage the ship loads of gold arriving from Europe. After this victory, Akbar also re-named his new city as Fatehpur.

The design of the Buland Darwaza deliberately accentuates the height and massive power of the gate and makes it visible from far. It is built of red sandstone with the decorations in white marble that lightens the impression of size when you are standing close to it. The expanse is broken by arched niches, small chhatris and marble highlights. It dominates the courtyard or *sahn* of the Jami Masjid. The principal arch stands in the centre of three projecting sides and topped by a dome. The lofty central arch is broken into three tiers with rows of smaller arches and flat brackets. Verses from the Quran have been carved in the delicate *naskh* script along the top and these were drawn by Khwaja Husain Chishti, a disciple of Sheikh Salim Chishti. Look up and you will see that the gate has many horse shoes nailed to the stone and many are also of draft cattle. Popular belief is that peasants used to pray to the Sheikh to cure their sick cattle which is reflected in the practice of tying threads at the shrine itself. One walks through a central hall below the dome of the gate and comes out into the main courtyard of the Jami Masjid.

◀ *The Buland Darwaza and one of the bastions of the outer wall.*

▶ *Akbar ordered the Buland Darwaza to be built after his conquest of Gujarat.*

Ibadat Khana

The building that has generated the most interest among experts is the Ibadat Khana, or house of worship where Akbar met philosophers and priests of every religion—mullahs and Jesuits, Brahmins, Buddhist monks and Zoroastrians and even an atheist or a hedonist. Later he unveiled his new faith the Din-i-Ilahi here before declaring it at the Friday prayers at the Jami Masjid. Built in 1575, this building rich in historical and literary traditions is mentioned by all the contemporary historians but none of them have identified it. Badauni writes that a cell used by a disciple of Salim Chishti was rebuilt and extended to create this hall. He wrote, 'Every Sabbath evening he invited sayyids, shaikhs, theologians and nobles, but ill feeling arose in the company about the order of precedence, so that his Majesty commanded that the nobles should sit on the east side, the sayyids on the west, the theologians on the south, and the sheikhs on the north. His Majesty would go to these various parties from time to time and converse with them to ascertain their thoughts.'

Historians do not agree on which of the many unnamed pavilions can be identified as this famous place. Some like Tillotson even speculate that it was the Diwan-i-Khas with Akbar sitting on top of his magnificent pillar to hold the sessions but that is dismissed by most historians. According to Rizvi, writing in the Archaeological Survey of India

◄ *A close-up of the varied forms of ornamentation on the gateway.*

handbook, it must have been near the imperial palaces so that Akbar could walk there easily. Also it would ideally have been near the mosque and the dargah of Salim Chishti. Another possibility is that the Ibadat Khana was demolished by some later Mughal king because he felt that Akbar's multi-religious discussions and debates were heretical activities.

Rizvi identifies the ruins of a building behind the main Haramsara that falls on the right as one leaves the royal enclosure to walk to the main gateway to the mosque. There is not much to see except a pile of rubble on a large platform and it

▲ *This square pavilion stands at the gate of Jodh Bai's Palace and was probably the quarters of the guards.*

takes some imagination to visualise the gatherings of priests and philosophers and the king wandering from group to group holding discussions. It was also the scene of passionate debates that it is said led to loud, dramatic arguments and people even coming close to blows. No one will really know where this house of worship actually stood.

There are many other structures scattered across the hill and one book lists 116 of them. Most

▲ *Stone Cutter's Mosque. An early version of the serpentine brackets can be seen here.*

of them are rows of rooms, wells and colonnades used for practical purposes like servants' quarters, stables and residences of officials. One interesting structure is the tower called the Hiran Minar where Akbar is said to have gone hunting deer. It is an Akash Diya, a tall light where lamps were hung from the rows of projecting sticks. Also the factories or karkhanas would have been nearby where according to Monserrate, 'are studios and workrooms for the finer and more reputable arts, such as paintings, goldsmith work, tapestry making, carpet and curtain making, and the manufacture of arms.'

The Stone Cutter's Mosque

This mosque stood at Sikri even before Akbar arrived there to meet the Sufi saint. Sikri's connection to Akbar started when he began to build the Agra Fort and much of the red sandstone came from the ridge at Sikri. So a group of stonecutters settled there and they were the first to discover and revere Sheikh Salim Chishti and in 1565 when the saint returned from a Haj, they built a mosque for their khwaja. If you study the carvings carefully you will notice a distinct difference in the quality of the work, some bits like the brackets are finely done while others are much cruder work. This shows that all the devout stonecutters did some work at the mosque. After the death of Salim Chishti the mosque was extended to include the Sheikh's cell.

▼ *Often a structure built in brick was given a facing in red sandstone.*

The mosque stands at the back of the Jami Masjid, behind a high enclosure and next to the area where the Sufi saint stayed. It has a nine arched facade and a richly ornamented *mihrab* and five bays using the deep red stone of Sikri. It is here that you will see an early version of the serpentine brackets that catch one's eye at the main mausoleum of the saint. Here they are in red sandstone and are a fine example of carving.

Rang Mahal

In 1569 when Akbar discovered that the Princess of Amber was with child he shifted her to Sikri to be near Salim Chishti. Rang Mahal or the Palace of Delight was built for the princess and her son Salim was born here and named after the saint. The palace was bought by the Government of India during the time of Lord Curzon but was in ruins and was even turned into a weaver's factory for some time. Much of the collapsed stone has been used elsewhere but still one can make out the shape and design of the palace that has such powerful historical resonance. There are patches of fine carvings like the floriated cusps of the arches emerging from the mouths of elephants. The

▼ *Rang Mahal. The first Akbari building at Fatehpur Sikri constructed for Mariam-us-Zamani.*

pillars have peacock tail bases and scalloped capitals. Looking at the piles of rubble and collapsed walls it is clear that the Rang Mahal has somehow not survived as well as the other royal buildings in Fatehpur Sikri.

Fatehpur Sikri after Akbar

In 1585 there were problems in the North-West Frontier and Akbar left the city with his army. From then on, he was on one campaign after another, battling Afghan tribes, conquering Kashmir and then Sind. All through this period he was based in Lahore and remained there till 1598. As the army and important officials had all accompanied him and were at Lahore, Fatehpur Sikri was deserted and many of the empty houses began to collapse. On his return Akbar stayed at the Agra Fort and soon the whole royal entourage had shifted back there. Fatehpur Sikri was in fact abandoned by the king. He was busy handling the rebellion of Prince Salim and at such a delicate juncture probably felt it more practical to live within the citadel at Agra that held his army and the royal treasury. He only stopped here for a very short visit in 1601 on his way back from the Deccan but never stayed here again.

Of the later Mughal kings, Jahangir took refuge here in 1619 when the plague raged in Agra. He celebrated the twenty-eighth birthday of his third son Prince Khurram here at this time and just for a few months the city once again saw a flash of

▶ *Selling religious mementoes to pilgrims.*

its old days of splendour but it was an ephemeral moment. The only people who remained were the descendants of Sheikh Salim Chishti. Some of them, the *sajjada-nashins*, were also among the nobility during Jahangir's reign. Fatehpur Sikri faced bad times when Aurangzeb moved on an endless campaign to the Deccan in 1681 and never came back, dying there in 1707. Both Agra and Fatehpur Sikri faced the predatory attacks of the Jats who took away marble, carvings and spoiled the palaces.

◀ *Jamaat Khana. The graves of the descendants of Salim Chishti.*

In the eighteenth century there was a flash of life when Muhammad Shah was crowned here in 1719. By then the Mughal Empire was on the path to disintegration. If anyone could have played blind man's buff in the Ankh Michauli palace and chess with living pieces it would have been this feckless king who was called 'Rangila' or the voluptuary. Slowly all the mansions crumbled to the ground, the city of hovels and huts vanished and all that remained was the main royal enclosure and the spiritual centre where the tomb of the saint continued to call the pilgrim.

Agra was seized by the East India Company in 1813 and the British entered the scene. By then the dried lake had been turned into fields and villages had grown where once bazaars had stood. The Chishti family suffered at the hands of the British because they had supported the uprising of 1857 and were reduced to poverty and most of the Sikri region turned into a slum. The British efforts at conserving the palaces were casual and at times thoughtless till Lord Curzon decided to save Agra and Fatehpur Sikri. The Public Works Department that had occupied many of the palaces was made to vacate them and the Viceroy made sure the palaces were repaired and maintained by the Archaeology Department. Once Akbar rode away from his city, Fatehpur Sikri never rose again. It still waits for his presence among the ghostly palaces, an unforgettable city frozen in time.

A COURTLY CITY FOR A KING

A courtly city for a king

'The colour tones became more subdued, lines more sure and subtle, expressions more lively and composition well-knit. The painters succeeded in a brilliant way in expressing the ideals of amity and synthesis preached by their imperial patron.'

-Asok Kumar Das

In many ways Akbar's years at Fatehpur Sikri were the richest and most productive of his reign. By then he was thirty years old and had built an empire over which he ruled with little opposition. So he built a city that reflected both his unquestioned power and also his cultural and religious interests. Akbar, a man who loved music, enjoyed painting and playing polo, built a courtly city not a fortress. Unlike the citadels of Agra and Lahore with their high forbidding walls and bastions this was the capital of a cultured monarch and maybe he was also completing Babur's dream of replicating Timur's Samarkand in India. Fatehpur Sikri was designed with an air of light heartedness as the playground of a king with not just soldier's barracks and a guarded treasury but also assigned spaces for artists and musicians, bathing pools for queens and princesses, polo grounds and elephant stables. It is an oddly delicate, artistic and playful construction.

The fifteen years at Fatehpur Sikri may have been brief but they were the best years of Akbar's nearly fifty-year reign as he matured both as a man and as a king. Reading the words of his finest biographer Abul Fazl, one senses a definite

◄ *No other Mughal fortress will have a building like the Panch Mahal.*

transformation as he became more contemplative and widened his interests. The mad rush to conquer, the avid hunger for land was abating and in the words of Abraham Eraly, 'his life became more and more austere, and he revealed himself to be a man of wide cultural interests and insatiable intellectual curiosity.' He was enjoying himself hugely and it was a time when every aspect of the life of his subjects and of the kingdom flourished under his nourishing beneficial eye. At Fatehpur Sikri it was as if nothing escaped the attention of Akbar who had a voracious curiosity about everything. From reforming the revenue system to building a library; patronising music and painting and devising newer ways to play polo. It then expanded to a growing interest in other religions, a deepening knowledge of philosophy and finally his evolving a new faith.

Many observers have commented on Akbar's prodigious energy and how he packed in an amazing

▼ *The wrongly credited palace of Birbal. Akbar's courtier would have built his haveli outside the citadel.*

amount of activities in the middle of all the burdens of running an empire. He was around to supervise the building work and many designs of palaces carry his unique touch. Monserrate even mentions him carrying baskets of earth and learning to carve stone. He was welcoming the best musicians like Mian Tansen and Baz Bahadur and the finest miniature painters of the land; encouraging the poetry of Faizi and the prose of his brother Abul Fazl; gathering together religious preachers and philosophers of every religion in the land for discussions in his Ibadat Khana and still finding time for a hunting expedition. Meanwhile three young princes were growing up in the harem and kings of other lands were sending their ambassadors with gifts and courteous messages of friendship. These years at Fatehpur Sikri were the golden years of Akbar's magnificent reign.

▼ *Khwabgah. Akbar's personal palace had many ornamental rooms used by a busy and social king.*

A People's King

Many observers have commented on how Akbar made himself accessible to his subjects, much more than later Mughal kings like Shah Jahan who chose to project a sort of divine detachment. It began with his showing himself to the common people every morning from his bedroom window in a ceremony he devised called Jharokha-i-Darshan and at that time the people gathered below his window were free to call out their requests. The public assembly at the Diwan-i-Aam was also open to everyone. Akbar was evolving into a king accepted by his subjects and the city plan of Fatehpur Sikri reflected this as it was designed as an open city, without any divisions.

The years of constant expansion were over and Akbar now got down to the business of consolidating his conquests through a reorganisation of the administration and the revenue system. It was not an easy task because after the death of Sher Shah Sur the administration had collapsed and Humayun had not lived long enough to revive it. First the system of surveying land and the collection of revenue was reorganised and then trade was actively encouraged with the building of highways lined with shady trees and caravanserais for travellers. Thomas Coryat, the eccentric English adventurer who walked to India during Jahangir's reign, declared that the highway connecting Lahore to Delhi and Agra was the best in the world. The irrigation systems were improved with the building of canals and lakes, and farmers were encouraged to increase their farm holdings by cutting down forests. Akbar was keen

'He has such a mastery of subtleties that he has introduced into India silken cloth, brocade, tapestry and carpet of silk and brocade...work in India has become much better than that of Persian and Europe...he has ordered that every story out of the three hundred and sixty stories of Amir Hamza be illustrated along with their episodes...it takes two years to prepare a volume and each volume entails an expenditure of about two lakh copper tankas.'

***Arif Qandhari** on Akbar's varied interests.*

to improve education and financed *pathshala*s and *madrassa*s. In all this, he was helped by an efficient team of officials led by the finance minister Raja Todar Mal, whose system of land survey and revenue assessment was so efficient that it was still in use four centuries later during the rule of the British.

Akbar had a supremely pragmatic attitude to life that was not influenced by either religion or social mores and he did not hesitate in addressing what he viewed as social evils even when it angered conservative people. He banned child marriages, setting the minimum age of marriage at fourteen for girls and sixteen for boys. He was deeply offended by the system of sati, where a Hindu widow was burnt on the funeral pyre of her husband, and abolished it and is quoted in the *Akbarnama*

◀ *The jharokha windows add a touch of ornamentation to the walls.*

as saying, 'It is an ancient custom in India for a women to burn herself on her husband's death, even though she may have been unhappy with him. And give up her priceless life with a cheerful countenance, conceiving it to be a means of her husband's salvation. It is a strange commentary on the magnanimity of men that they should seek their deliverance by means of their wives.' He even persuaded a princess of Bikaner not to commit Sati for the sake of her young children.

▲ *The courtyard, colonnade and garden before the Diwan-i-Aam.*

Living in the City

What was it like to live in a new city like Fatehpur Sikri? The idea of city planning did not exist at this time and what usually happened was that the king built his citadel and then the nobility, the omrahs, built their mansions in the outer peripheries, just beyond the citadel walls. One broad street usually led off the main gate and there were shops on

▲ *View from the royal complex when walking towards the mosque and the dargah.*

both sides of it, with the traders living on the upper floors. Then the rest of the city grew in a rather a disorganised manner with ordinary people building their thatched huts in a jumble along narrow, winding streets, very much like modern day slums. Even though Fatehpur Sikri was a new city, any section where the poor lived would not have been a pretty sight. As Abraham Eraly describes it, Mughal cities were 'at once thriving and decrepit, magnificent and squalid'.

India had known urban planning during the time of the Indus Valley Civilisation when Mohenjodaro and Harrapa were built around 1500 BCE and even at the time of the Mauryan capital of Pataliputra in the third century BCE. But by the time of Akbar, cities had no overall plan and this was partly because the concept of a capital of a kingdom was

rather vague. The capital was where the king was, as the whole government machinery moved with him. There were important cities like Agra, Delhi, Lahore and Fatehpur Sikri but none of them could be designated as the capital. For instance all through the years that Akbar was in Fatehpur Sikri, the main garrison guarding the royal treasury was still stationed at Agra Fort and most of the trade and industry also remained there. Only the nobility moved to the new city with the king, with all the people attached to the royal household including the bureaucracy, servants, soldiers, shops and craftsmen moving with them.

▲ *View of the citadel from the road to Agra.*

In its heyday Fatehpur Sikri had the citadel on top of the hill, with the mansions—the havelis of the omrahs, placed along the slope of the hill and below would be the chaotic jumble of huts and houses where ordinary people lived. Today the havelis and the homes of the poor that were made of mud brick have all vanished and only the stone palaces of the royal enclosure have survived. A small settlement of Sikri still survives in the shadow of the gateway of the Buland Darwaza, at the bottom of the hill, where descendants of the craftsmen of those times still weave dhurries and carve stone. The narrow winding lanes and their brick-built, whitewashed homes probably differ little from those built during the time of Akbar.

▼ *Many nameless ruins surround the palaces and these may have been stables or housed soldiers or craftsmen.*

As one drives up the hill to the main gateway of the citadel one can still see the remains of shops on both sides. Once this must have been the main thoroughfare like Chandni Chowk is to the Red Fort in Delhi. Stop and look at the desolate stone and try to imagine what it must have been like when Akbar was living in the palaces beyond. The shops would have been shaded by colourful awnings and sold everything from gold, jewels and carpets to grain, pottery, textiles and furniture. At regular intervals there would have been busy caravanserais, the inns

welcoming visitors from Persia and China and many food shops filled with the smoke of cooking. The road lined with shady trees would be filled with people, horses, elephants, bullock carts and palanquins and the air echoing to the call of vendors selling fruits and vegetables, fresh fish from the lake, trinkets, caps, shoes and sherbets ... All is silent now.

Royal Luxury and Plebeian Misery

Once past the gateway, and within Akbar's regal world, life in the palaces was one of luxurious ease and comfort. Here all activities were centred about the person of the king and the rhythms of the day were set by his schedules. There were the daily ceremonials of the public and private audiences and there was a busy calendar of festivals and feasts.

◀ *The Badshahi Darwaza was named after the king as it was used by Akbar.*

Akbar was known to be strict about expenses, even then the imperial budget for the household has been calculated at Rs. 4.7 million per year! Of course money was never a problem with Akbar as his treasury overflowed with gold and silver and his extravagant lifestyle was copied by his nobles who vied with each other to imitate him. For instance, Akbar got a thousand sets of clothes stitched every year, many of them were gifted to guests, so his historian Abul Fazl would give away all his clothes to the poor every year. The king often sat down to a meal of over two hundred dishes, Fazl was also famous for a *dastarkhwan* or spread of a hundred dishes.

The population of the city would have been a majority of Hindus and with the upper crust made up mostly by Muslims, Persians, Turks and Afghans with a sprinkling of Rajputs, Parsis and Europeans. The city really survived by catering to the extravagant demands of the royal family and the omrah and that was quite an extensive market. Just Akbar's harem was said to have five thousand women including queens, princesses, concubines, female relatives and an army of servants. The daily audiences were scenes of pageantry and even more so were the festivals and celebrations with people in silks and jewels and endless menus of expensive dishes, and

▶ *The courtyard of Jodh Bai's Palace was once the scene of colourful festivals and celebrations.*

◀ *The Panch Mahal was connected to the Haramsara for the use of the royal women.*

entertainment by singers and dancers. The wealth of the Mughals was unimaginable, and the Dutch traveller Francisco Pelsaert writes that at Akbar's death the royal treasury held seven million gold mohurs, one hundred million silver rupees, 230 million copper dams and gems, ornaments and more gold and silver in bullion.

It was in many ways an empty show of glamour as the condition of the poor was pathetic and peasants considered themselves lucky if they could feed their families. It was an economy based on exploitation where every level of society exploited the layer below and it ended with a peasantry deeply burdened with taxes. At times Akbar tried to alleviate their condition but the whole economic structure was flawed, discouraging enterprise in any form. As Pelsaert writes, 'In the palaces of these lords dwells all the wealth there is, wealth which glitters indeed but is ... wrung from the sweat of the poor ... resting on no firm foundation... (though) resplendent in the eyes of the world.' The king and the nobility were indifferent to the development of either agriculture or industry and the difference in the economic state of the rich and poor was shocking. So most of the ordinary people to be seen in the streets of Fatehpur Sikri would have been underfed and barely clad and they would have lived in hovels bare of any furniture and with few possessions. The lucky ones found employment in the palaces and mansions, the rest barely survived. All the glitter was around the king and the rest was darkness.

▲ *The pavilion to the left is called the Abdar Khana where the king's drinking water was stored.*

A Matter of Faith

The years at Fatehpur Sikri were comparatively free from wars and for the first time since he became king, Akbar had the time to indulge his curiosity about religion and philosophy. From being a restless, physical, sportsman he was evolving into a much more contemplative and intellectual man. From his childhood he had been fascinated by faqirs, yogis and Sufi pirs and loved listening to the religious writings of Hafiz and Rumi. For such an ambitious, hard driving man he had an odd melancholic aspect to his character. At times he would withdraw from people to spend time in meditation seeking answers to metaphysical questions about existence and the meaning of life. Badauni writes that he 'would sit many a morning alone in prayer and meditation, on a large flat stone in a lonely spot.' For a medieval monarch Akbar was surprisingly free of religious

◀ *Interiors of the Jami Masjid.*

prejudices and would accept any philosophy that attracted him. One great influence on him was Abul Fazl's father Sheikh Mubarak, a Sufi philosopher who had introduced the king to the concept of Sulh-i-kul, a belief in universal tolerance and peace. Fortuitously, this came at a time when the king was seeking ways to unite his diverse subjects under Mughal hegemony and Sulh-i-kul was a religiously tolerant, caste-free creed that was humane and could become a uniting force. Also through this belief the king could become the centre of people's faith. He was also attracted to the rituals and beliefs of other faiths and became a worshipper of the sun like the Hindus and kept a sacred fire like the Zoroastrians while also joining in celebrating Hindu festivals like Deepavali and the Parsi new year of Navroze. A true renaissance man, he kept his hair long like his Hindu ministers and at times wore a dhoti and put the dot of tilak on his forehead.

One of the mysteries of Fatehpur Sikri is the location of Akbar's House of Worship that he called Ibadat Khana. Some historians feel it was the palace we now call Diwan-i-Aam and others look for it among the ruins beyond the Jami Mosque. All Abul Fazl tells us is that Akbar built the Ibadat Khana in 1575 where initially he only invited Muslim mullahs but they shocked and disappointed the king by their unseemly quarrels. Even Badauni, who was suspicious of Akbar's pantheistic interests, writes critically of how the Shia and Sunni mullahs nearly came to blows over small matters like the seats and the order of precedence. So the king widened the field and included men from every religion—Hindus, Jains, Zoroastrians, Jews, Christians, even a few members of the Hindu sect of atheists called Nastikas and the hedonistic Charvakas who believed in leading a life of pleasure.

It must have been an interesting gathering with the king wandering from group to group asking

'The king's own palace is the largest and finest. The second palace belongs to the queens, and the third to the royal princes, whilst the fourth is used as a store house and royal magazine.'...'The roofs of these palaces are not tiled but dome shaped, being protected from the weather on the outside by solid plaster covering the stone slabs. The palaces are decorated also with many pinnacles, supported on four columns, each of which forms a small covered portico.'

***Antonio Monserrate**, the Portuguese Jesuit who lived at Akbar's court in Fatehpur Sikri on the palaces.*

questions and starting off discussions. What is amusing is that his genuine curiosity made many of the preachers believe they were close to converting the king, especially the Jesuits from Portugal who were convinced they were close to saving the soul of Akbar. As a matter of fact no one was very sure what he believed in because for this remarkably tolerant and intellectually curious man, faith was a surprisingly fluid concept. Till the end he remained a practising Muslim but what he refused to accept was the unquestioned authority of the ulema, the Muslim priesthood and it gained him their virulent opposition.

To everyone's surprise, in 1582 Akbar unveiled a new faith that he called Din-i-Ilahi or the religion

◀ *A variety of ornamental styles were used in the interiors of the mosque.*

of god at Fatehpur Sikri. It was an eclectic mix of all that he had heard in the Ibadat Khana that had appealed to him. It was also an attempt to create a faith that could calm the religious unrest prevailing among his subjects by making the king both the temporal and religious head of the state and he even began to read the prayers at the mosque as its chief propagator. According to Abul Fazl, 'he is a man who makes justice the guide of the path of enquiry, and takes from every sect what is consonant with reason'. He was creating a liberal, reasonable, inclusive faith that was an idealised collection of his socio-political beliefs. Din-i-Ilahi had no priesthood, no holy book and was based on the Sufi idea of the absorption of the soul in the Divine Being. The ulema were outraged when he stamped his coins with the phrase 'Allahu Akbar' which means 'God is Great' but could also be interpreted as Akbar is God! The king never bothered to clarify the matter of course.

As a new faith Din-i-Ilahi did not last beyond its founder's life. Only a few members of his closest circle of friends like Birbal, Abul Fazl and Faizi joined it while other members of the elite like Man Singh and Todar Mal courteously refused. Even his family showed little interest and none of the Mughal kings who followed ever spoke of Akbar's inclusive but slightly eccentric faith. However what it did do was imbue life in Fatehpur Sikri with a sense of openness and creative discovery. From the new styles evolving in the studios of the miniature painters to the compositions of Tansen and Baz Bahadur, the new craft of Persian carpet weaving that was introduced by Akbar to evolving a new Indian style of carving. The king and his faith created an ambience of liberal humanity that made Fatehpur Sikri a unique culturally vibrant and colourfully courtly city. It reflected the life and mind of the king in a way few other cities have done in India. To understand Akbar you have to wander around the palaces of his dream city and let him take over your imagination.

The Royal Historian

Akbar wanted a proper history of the Mughals to be written, so he encouraged members of his family and the court to write down their own memoirs. Among them were his aunt Gulbadan and two servants of Humayun—Jauhar and Bayazid. We know so much about Akbar's reign because all the events were recorded in meticulous detail by his historian Abul Fazl Allami. His two mammoth chronicles, the *Akbarnama* or the History of Akbar and the Ain-i-Akbari or the Regulations of Akbar are the best source of information on his reign. Being official histories they are of course full of flowery praise of the king who, in Abul Fazl's adoring eyes, could do no wrong. At the same time another scholar Badauni was secretly writing his *Muntakhab-ut-Tawarikh*, a bitter, highly critical and jaundiced account that is very amusing to read and does balance Fazl's worshipful words. Badauni, who was rather a religious bigot felt slighted by the king's favours to Fazl and seldom found anything about Akbar worth praising.

At Fatehpur Sikri, Akbar also indulged in his passion for books. During his childhood he had not bothered much with his lessons and was in fact only semi-literate and there is only one document that carries his signature, a childish scrawl that he must have been deeply embarrassed about. Fortunately

a medieval monarch did not need to be a scholar and when he discovered the pleasure of books, he got people to read them to him and because of his prodigious memory gained much from them. His magnificent personal library held over twenty thousand manuscripts and he established a department of calligraphers and painters who copied out manuscripts and then these were illustrated with miniature paintings. Sanskrit works like the *Mahabharata* were translated at his orders and he was fond of listening to the stories of the epic that he called *Razmnama*, the tales of the Great War.

Bejewelled Books

For Akbar a book meant a manuscript with the text written in elegant calligraphy, with full page illustrations in an iridescent palette of colours and borders decorated in gold and silver patterns. A miniature painting was done on many varied subjects. It could show the king in his durbar surrounded by the omrah in gorgeous clothes and dancing women; a battle scene with horses and elephants and charging soldiers; rather gory hunting scenes; the siege of a fort or illustrate a love story with the lovers cavorting in a garden. A medieval manuscript was a work of art and at Fatehpur Sikri the calligraphists and miniature painters produced some of the finest books of the Mughal period. Abul Fazl calls the atelier where the

◀ *Many religious quotations are carved on the Buland Darwaza.*

▲ *Wall paintings that reflect the floral motifs used in miniature paintings.*

calligraphers and painters worked the Tasvirkhana, the painter's bureau and it shows Akbar's personal interest in paintings. The Kitabkhana was the library where these manuscripts were preserved for the king.

The art of miniature painting practised in Persia was introduced into India by Akbar's father Humayun. At the time when he had taken refuge in the court of the Shah of Persia he had employed two Safavid artists Mir Sayyid Ali and Abdus Samad and these two men followed him to India. As a boy in Kabul, Akbar learnt painting from them and then when he set up a painter's workshop at Fatehpur Sikri they took over the day to day running of the studio. The king took a personal interest in the Tasvirkhana and often visited it to study the progress of the manuscripts. As historian Andrew Topsfield writes about the products of the studio, 'Like much else in Mughal India, the imperial style was above all the creation of the energetic personality of Akbar.' He

explains the style further and writes, 'Under Akbar's close supervision, a vigorous style of epic and poetical manuscript illustration was rapidly formed, which combined Persian technical refinement with Indian intensity and feeling for nature.'

The painters who worked here were mostly Indian and they brought an Indian sensibility to the art and created a style that was uniquely Mughal. These Indian painters, in the words of A. K. Das, 'reveal a sense of realism and authenticity, witnessed or experienced by the painters themselves ... The portraits are life like, the architectural details contemporary and the flora and fauna and landscape in most examples authentic.' Among the painters whose names can be found on the paintings are Basawan, Daswant, Mukund, Kesu and Lal. Akbar who was always in search of talent, himself discovered Daswant who was the son of a poor *kahar*, a palanquin bearer and as a boy he used to draw on stray walls of the city.

A miniature painting was created by a team of painters with a senior artist designing and sketching the picture with another painting the faces and a third filling in the colours. A complete book with calligraphy and painting took years to complete and were precious possessions. Among the manuscripts the most celebrated, with 1200 illustrations was the *Dastan-e-Amir Hamza* that told the adventures of the hero Amir Hamza. The *Mahabharata* was translated into Persian with the title *Razmnama*, also the *Tutinama*, with folk tales. Then there was the autobiography of Babur, the *Baburnama* and the history of his son in the *Humayunama*. The finest paintings can be seen in the history of Akbar's reign, the *Akbarnama*. At least four copies of Abul Fazl's classic were made and the best preserved folio is now in the Victoria and Albert Museum in London.

The Karkhanas of Sikri

A number of production centres for the decorative arts, called *karkhanas*, were also established at Fatehpur Sikri and they met the demands of the royal establishment. There were karkhanas of silk and cotton weavers, wood carvers, potters, metal workers and, jewellers. The toshkhana was where the textiles–cotton, silk, velvet and brocades were kept and the farrashkhana was where Persian carpets were woven and stored. Akbar is credited with introducing the craft of carpet weaving in the country by getting Persian weavers to come and settle here. Here the giant tents were also made that were required when the king and his family was on the move and a travelling city went with him. It is said that the great imperial tents took a thousand workers a week to erect. Father Monserrate describes what he saw here, 'studios and work-rooms for finer and more reputable arts, such as paintings, goldsmith-work, tapestry-making, carpet-and-curtain-making, and the manufacture of arms.' Many writers mention these karkhanas but unfortunately none of them give their exact location and archaeologist can only guess where they stood.

Babur and Humayun did not get the opportunity to lay the foundation of the Mughal tradition of arts and crafts, this was left to Akbar. He had a voracious interest in every aspect of life and after years of conquests and the consolidation of the empire it was at Fatehpur Sikri that he got the opportunity to focus on the pleasures of building a library or planning the decor of the palaces. Of the Mughal artefacts that have survived few can be dated with certainty to the reign of Akbar but one has to just study the miniature paintings to get a sense of the delicately woven textiles, the fine workmanship of the jewellery or the swords and shield, the wooden furniture inlaid with mother-of-pearl, marble inlaid with semi-precious stones, ceramics, jade, crystal and in the interior scenes the bejewelled colours of the carpets that still dazzle the eye.

A description of a royal procession gives us an idea of the kind of crafts that were the decorative part of the pageantry of Akbar's life. Here is Badauni writing about Akbar going out in procession to welcome Sulaiman Mirza the ruler of Badakhshan, 'On that day 5000 elephants, some with housings of European velvet, and some with Turkish cloth of gold, and some with chains of gold and silver and, with black and white fringes hung on their heads and necks, were drawn up in line on both sided. Also Arabian and Persian horses with golden saddles of splendour. And between each pair of elephants they placed a car of cheetahs with golden collars, and coverings of velvet and fine linen, and an oxen car with fillets of embroidered gold.'

▶ *The adorning of walls will reach its zenith with the inlay on marble at the Taj Mahal.*

The Navaratnas

The tradition of important courtiers in a king's court being referred to as 'gems' or 'jewels' is an old one in India. In the Gupta period, sixth century AD, the legendary King Chandragupta Vikramaditya is said to have had nine courtiers called the *navaratnas* including the poet Kalidas, the physician Dhanvantri and the astronomer Varahamihira. In the sixteenth century, around the time of Babur, King Krishnadeva Raya of Vijayanagar had eight such men called the *ashtadiggajas* including the poets Allasani Pedanna and Tenali Raman.

So the tradition of men being termed as 'gems' or 'jewels' when appearing regularly in a king's entourage continued in Mughal times where important courtiers in Fatehpur Sikri were referred to as one of the navaratnas. However we have to remember these were just their reputations among the people and they were not assigned their astral roles by the king! Nowhere in the chronicles of the period are the navaratnas mentioned by name and most tellingly Abul Fazl, himself often topping the list, never mentions it in his monumental history. Akbar probably never knew he had so many jewels in his court.

Also when you actually get down to listing their names, finding nine of them becomes quite difficult as most lists reach up to seven and then become rather confused. Usually these seven are Abul Fazl, Faizi, Birbal, Man Singh, Abdur Rahim, Todar Mal and Tansen. After

▶ *This was the residence of Akbar's senior queens Ruquaiyya Begum and Salima Sultan and not Birbal.*

that, at times, a Faqir Aziao-Din is mentioned but nothing is known about him except that he was a scholar. And finally for the ninth some mention Mulla Do Piaza who as far as I know was a fictional creation to act as the butt of Birbal's jokes! Other speculative names include the singer Baz Bahadur and the miniature painters Abdus Samad and Mir Sayyid Ali but in fact what we really have are seven members of the court at Fatehpur Sikri who have been credited as an Akbari jewel. Also what is intriguing is that at a time when close to eighty percent of the nobility, the omrahs, was Muslim, four out of these seven are Hindus. So may be the term should not be taken so literally.

ABUL FAZL (1551-1602) and his elder brother FAIZI (1547-95) were the sons of Sheikh Mubarak, a Sufi preacher who influenced Akbar's philosophical thinking. The brothers were closely associated with Akbar's policy of religious toleration and the promulgation of his faith Din-i-Ilahi. Both were prodigies and Faizi was honoured as the poet laureate and was famous for his *ghazals* and *qasidas*. He also translated tales from the *Mahabharata*, wrote a treatise on the Vedanta and books on mathematics. Abul Fazl's magnum opus was the *Akbarnama*, the official history of Akbar's reign and the *Ain-i-Akbari* that is, in the words of Bamber Gascoigne, 'an astounding combination of gazetteer, almanac, dictionary of science, book of rules and procedures, and statistical digest' and is full of fascinating information about the royal establishment. What makes this history unique is that

Abul Fazl brought a systematic approach to the writing of history, where facts were checked and an effort made to provide correct information. The brothers were trusted courtiers and friends of the king and Akbar was devastated when his eldest son Prince Salim, who was leading a rebellion, was found responsible for the assassination of Abul Fazl.

RAJA BIRBAL (1528-53) was born Mahesh Das in a middle class Brahmin family in a Madhya Pradesh village and was part of the entourage from Amber. He caught Akbar's eye through his intelligence and sharp wit. Today the many apocryphal tales woven around Akbar and Birbal make him into a sort of court jester but he was in fact a trusted adviser and close confidant of the king. He was given the title of Raja and tradition says that the name Birbal, meaning a powerful mind, was also conferred on him by Akbar. He was a poet, with the title of Kavi Priya, and wrote under the pen name of 'Brahma'. Birbal was killed in a battle while leading an army in the North-West Frontier.

TANSEN (1506-89) was born Ramtanu Pandey in a village near Satna in Madhya Pradesh. His father was a singer in a temple in Varanasi and noticing the musical talent of his young son he took him to Swami Haridas, a famous singer and religious teacher in Vrindavan. After his tutelage with Haridas the young Ramtanu was taught by the Sufi preacher and musician Muhammad Ghaus of Gwalior. Haridas was a Bhakti poet and Ghaus was a Sufi so Ramtanu was imbued with a liberal creed that sang of devotion and tolerance. He married Ghaus' daughter Hussaini and remained a spiritual free thinker. His fame as a singer of dhrupad grew as the court singer of Raja Ramchandra of Rewa and he was given the title of Tansen. At this time Akbar heard of him and sent a request that Tansen be sent to Fatehpur Sikri and the raja could hardly refuse. Here Tansen became a legend, affectionately called 'Miyan' by a king who loved music and he is credited with many famous ragas like Miyan ki Malhar and Darbari Kanada. It is said that the stone seat in the middle of the pool called Anup Talao was where Tansen stood to sing to his monarch.

▶ *Akbar would spend congenial moments at the Khwabgah with his courtiers and friends like Birbal, Abul Fazl and Faizi.*

ABDUR RAHIM was a poet, bureaucrat and soldier. He was the son of Bairam Khan who was Akbar's guardian and regent and was adopted by Akbar at his father's death. Abdur Rahim became a part of the royal family when Akbar married his mother Salima Sultan. He was the senior-most minister at Fatehpur Sikri with the title of Khan-i-Khanan and was a popular poet. His pithy couplets written under the pen name 'Rahim' are still remembered and Indian children still learn them in school. Abdur Rahim's mausoleum stands in the shadow of Humayun's Tomb, near the Nizamuddin Dargah in Delhi.

RAJA MAN SINGH headed the Rajput conclave in the court at Fatehpur Sikri. He was the Raja of Amber (modern Jaipur), the nephew of the queen Mariam-us-Zamani (Jodh Bai) and a famous general who was often sent off to handle important military campaigns. He was given the title of Amir-ul-omara and appointed the governor of the important province of Bengal.

RAJA TODAR MAL was a Hindu from Punjab who became Akbar's finance minister and developed the Mughal revenue system that lasted till the British times. It was based on meticulous land surveys and the classification of land according to production. As the rate of revenue was fixed, it rose dramatically and was responsible for the prosperity of the Mughals. He was given the title of Raja for his administrative and military abilities.

These were men of many parts because in Mughal times you had to be both courtier and warrior to rise in the bureaucracy and Akbar enjoyed the company of creative minds. Birbal, Abdur Rahim and Abul Fazl were poets and writers who acted as diplomats and led the army. Todar Mal was not just an administrator and revenue specialist but also a very successful military general. And Man Singh was interested in architecture and built many temples and the delightful Amber Fort that still looms over the city of Jaipur, its mellow golden walls shimmering in the sun. Like their irrepressibly talented patron, Akbar's jewels were remarkable men.

◀ *Todar Mal's Pavilion. Todar Mal created the taxation system that was used by all Mughal kings.*

The Battle for the Dargah

When Emperor Akbar assigned the revenue of seven villages for the upkeep of the Dargah of Sheikh Salim Chishti at Fatehpur Sikri he could not possibly have imagined the conflict and confusion that would follow. Three hundred and fifty years after the death of Akbar, the Mughal dynasty came to an end after the Uprising of 1857. That was when the last Mughal king Bahadur Shah II was banished to Rangoon for leading a mutiny by the sepoys of the English army. Soon after the Dargah at Fatehpur Sikri came into prominence again as the descendents of the Sufi saint began a bitter and long drawn battle for his legacy. And going through the voluminous official papers of the Office of the Commissioner of Agra, the dispute over the religious endowment of the shrine was still going on eighty years later in 1939, producing a small mountain of paper and no end in sight.

It all begins with a gentleman called Abdul Hai who was the Sajjada-nashin or the keeper of the shrine in 1857. When the sepoys rose in rebellion against their English masters at Meerut, they immediately rode to Delhi and barged into the Red Fort where Bahadur Shah was spending his last peaceful days. The Mughal king was over eighty years old and a reluctant leader of the rebels who once again declared him the Badshah of Hindustan. The rebellion spread quickly and, as far as one can make out from the rather laconic notes of the British officials, one band of sepoys from the army camp at Nimuch, arrived at Fatehpur Sikri and forced poor Abdul Hai to join them. Hai disappeared and after the uprising came to an end

▶ *The dargah has survived many years of neglect because of the presence of the pilgrims.*

he was declared an offender by the English and Akbar's religious endowment was taken away. Reading behind the rather dry words in the files one finds the hidden story of poor Abdul Hai and the impossible situation that he faced during those chaotic and dangerous days. In the words of a sympathetic official, the 'offence of the Sajjada-nashin Abdul Hai was personal. (He) was forced to rebel under direct pressure and that he was admittedly

the victim of circumstances—when the government officials had been compelled to abandon the place by the Nimuch mutineers at the beginning of July 1857. It was impossible to expect the Sajjada-nashin to take the part of the government in the face of more than 2,000 armed men, aided by all the turbulent people of the countryside.' Hai seemed to have returned a few years later and was given amnesty by the government after he explained his dilemma and he was allowed to go on living at Sikri.

However the knotty question of the endowment remained. Abdul Hai was not allowed to manage it any longer and so he put forward the claims of his son but by then there were rival demands from every conceivable descendant of Salim Chishti. In the late nineteenth century the total amount of money under dispute was about Rs. 11,000 rupees, quite a substantial sum for the time and so worth the battle. And battle they did, with a fierce tenacity typical of Indians and with a blizzard of petitions and appeals. The correspondence would finally involve the Collector of Sikri, the Commissioner of the Agra Division, the Office of the Accountant General, the Chief Secretary of the United Provinces, the Board of Revenue, the Public Works Department and the Archaeology Department. All patiently handling appeals from men claiming to be the rightful Sajjada-nashin and to spice up the brew there was now a Muslim Committee appointed to oversee the running of the shrine and they wanted their piece of the pie.

The tricky question was how to disburse the funds to pay for the repair of the buildings, the salaries of the *khadims*, (caretakers), and the running of a *tahsili* school. The Muslim Committee was deeply unhappy at the way the funds were being used and felt the upkeep of the shrine was being neglected. The Archaeology Department felt that the money could be used better by them to maintain the buildings in the mosque area. And all the Chishti descendants were also fighting over who had the right to be buried inside Islam Khan's Tomb within the mosque precinct where traditionally the Sajjada-nashin was laid to rest.

So there were petitions, appeals for scholarships, legal notices, minutes of meetings, starred questions in the UP Legislative Assembly, letters, wills, voter's lists and a case filed in the Allahabad High Court. And at the receiving end of all this was the hapless Commissioner of Agra and over the years one finds many of them making a futile attempt to bring the dispute to an end. There is W H L Impey trying to make sense of it all in 1901 and writing, 'The delay in its submission is due to the fact that many of the papers required for reference could not be traced in my office and I have only lately received from the Collector a mass of old papers dealing with the question.' One can see poor Impey sitting with a pile of yellowing files full of undecipherable notations and trying to make some sense of them all. As he goes on patiently, 'The subject matter of the petition is a very old one, and has been frequently considered by the local officers and by the government at various times during the last 50 years.'

Then with a touch of exasperation he continues, 'The descendants of Sheikh Salim Chishti are divided into two branches, which have for many generations been on bad terms with each other (1) the descendants in the male line now represented by the present Sajjada-nashin Abdul Aziz and (2) the descendants of the Sheikh's daughter, represented by Tajammul Husain.' Later in the papers one discovers more claimants, including a branch of the family that had moved to Delhi centuries ago and now suddenly woke up to their legacy. Most interesting were a couple of gentlemen who belonged to the Shia faith; they had bought a share in the endowment from some member of the Chishti family who were in fact Sunnis. And so it goes on...

What was fascinating about dipping into these papers are the titbits of information about Fatehpur Sikri in the nineteenth century. A persistent collector had even discovered the list of the original seven villages endowed by Akbar in 1570—Jajau, Mahadau, Sirabli, Bharauti, Mai Buzurg, Nagla Bharauti and Arazi Imlak. What is intriguing is that a list of fifty-eight villages in the area in 1927 contains the name of four of them. Then we discover that, rather appropriately, scholar and historian Abul Fazl's house 'at the back of Sheikh Salim Chishti's tomb' was being used as the school. Here the Persian teacher was being paid Rs. 20 per month when the poor English teacher was only getting Rs. 15 and the total expenditure of running the school was a princely Rs. 600 a year.

As they did everywhere in India, the British officials had a propensity for using the Mughal palaces as their official residences and the Archaeology Department did not always approve. As one acerbic note in 1900 says, 'That rules as to the reservations of Birbal's house for "District Officers" and "distinguished travellers" and of Miriam's house for officers of the Public Works Department should be rigorously enforced, and that all other persons should be required to go to the dak bungalow.' Akbar's Daftar Khana was similarly being used by visiting bureaucrats and one can imagine the scene of the red faced Collector stomping into a pillared Mughal pavilion yelling 'Koi hai!' and demanding a chhota peg from the khansama. The dak bungalow, by the way, had a butler!
Of course the fact that these buildings were used may have helped in their survival because the description of the state of Salim Chishti's shrine that was in the hands of Indians makes one cringe. This is a note by E Rose, Commissioner of Agra writing in 1899, 'It is most desirable that responsible custodians should be placed in charge of the buildings. I found several places in which the marble tracery had been designedly chipped off, and Mr Smith of the Archaeological Survey informed me a few days ago that some of the horse shoes of historical interest, which are affixed to the doors of the great gateway, had been removed. The walls have been disfigured in many places by visitors who have considered it necessary to record their names and the date of their visit ... during the cold weather the place is thronged by unfortunate and persistent mendicants and by hungry set of imposters who profess to be guides.' Then during an annual fair, 'I found furnaces and native fireplaces in all parts of the quadrangle and a huge halwai's shop with big fires at work.' Such official comments about the sad state of the shrine with dirty floors covered in pigeon droppings, broken marble screens, the Buland Darwaza area being turned into an open air toilet and the deterioration of the mother of pearl catafalque go on till the end.

One wonders what Akbar and the ascetic Sheikh would have thought of this endless family conflict over money. And as it was all across India, we have much to thank the British and their conscientious preservation of Indian monuments. The legacy of Akbar and Salim Chishti at Fatehpur Sikri was preserved not by the people entrusted with the responsibility but by the officials of the British Government.

INDEX

GETTING THERE

The nearest city is Agra, Uttar Pradesh. Fatehpur Sikri is 37 km from Agra and an hour's drive away. Agra is 224 km from Delhi.

By air

The nearest domestic airport is at Agra. The nearest international airport is at Delhi.

By road

Excellent luxury bus connections from Delhi, the trip takes about five hours. You can also hire a car and visit Mathura on the way. Jaipur is a six hour bus journey.

By train

The fastest trains from Delhi are the Shatabdi and the Taj Express, both take you to Agra in time for a day of sightseeing and the trains leave for Delhi in the evening. Stay overnight at Agra and spend an entire day at Fatehpur Sikri.

Best time to visit

October to March. December-January requires heavy woollens.

Other nearby places worth visiting

Mathura and Vrindavan on the Delhi-Agra highway. Mathura has an excellent museum with an amazing collection of Buddhist and Hindu sculptures of the Gupta period.